HOW TO
WRITE
& MARKET
YOUR
MYSTERY NOVEL

MYSTERIES BY JEAN HAGER

Mitch Bushyhead Series

The Grandfather Medicine
Night Walker
Ghostland
The Fire Carrier
Masked Dancers

Molly Bearpaw Series

Ravenmocker
The Redbird's Cry
Seven Black Stones
The Spirit Caller

Iris House Bed and Breakfast Series

Blooming Murder
Dead and Buried
Death on the Drunkard's Path
The Last Noel
Sew Deadly

Single Titles

Terror in the Sunlight
Evil Side of Eden
Shadow of the Tamaracks
Dangerous Enchantment

HOW TO WRITE & MARKET YOUR MYSTERY NOVEL

A Step-by-Step Guide From Idea to Final Rewrite and Marketing

Jean Hager

Southmont Publishing
P. O. Box 33024
Tulsa, OK 74153-1024

How to Write & Market Your Mystery Novel.
Copyright © 1998 by Jean Hager.
Printed and bound in the United States of America. All rights
reserved. No part of this book may be reproduced in any form
or by any electronic or mechanical means including information
storage and retrieval systems without permission in writing from
the publisher, except by a reviewer, who may quote brief
passages in a review. Published by Southmont Publishing,
P. O. Box 33024, Tulsa, OK 74153-1024.

First edition.

Library of Congress Cataloging in Publication Data

Hager, Jean.
    How to write & market your mystery novel : a step-by-step
    guide from idea to final rewrite and marketing / Jean Hager.
    — 1st ed.
      p.cm.
    Includes bibliographical references and index.
    LCCN: 97-91382

      1. Detective and mystery stories—Authorship. 2.
    Authorship—Marketing. 3. Book industries and trade. 4.
    Authors and publishers. I. Title. II. Title: How to write and
    market your mystery novel
    PN3377.5.D4H34 1998   808.3'872
                           QB197-41485
    ISBN 0-9662145-0-1

To order this book from the publisher, include $3.00 postage for 1
book and 50 cents for each additional book. Quantity discounts are
available on bulk purchases for educational, business, or sales
promotional use. For information, please contact Southmont
Publishing, P. O. Box 33024, Tulsa, OK 74153-1024. 800-550-7741

CONTENTS

INTRODUCTION

There are good reasons for writing a genre novel like a mystery, rather than a mainstream book—especially for a beginning novelist. (Mainstream novels are books shelved under "Fiction" in bookstores and identified as "Fiction" on the spine.) Any novel that can't be packaged with a genre label—mystery, romance, western, etc.—can be called a mainstream novel. Some are literary, some commercial, some good, some bad. The label has nothing to do with the quality of the book.

Genre novels enjoy a sizable readership. Why are they so popular? One reason is that they reaffirm beliefs or ideals held by a large percentage of the population. Take romances, a popular genre. People who read them believe that ideally true love overcomes all obstacles and lasts forever. Even when it hasn't turned out that way in their own experience, it has for other people and they continue to hope it can happen—or *ought* to—when they meet the right person. In a romance novel, the hero and heroine may have had past relationships, even marriages, but they never found the one person in the world meant for them until they found each other. Romance novels reaffirm the belief in a happily-ever-after love. Obviously this is a widely held belief since more romances are sold than any other type of novel.

Two other popular genres, westerns and mysteries, plug into some of the same widely held beliefs as to how things *ought* to be. When evil tears the fabric of a society, it ought to be exposed and eradicated, so that society can be put right again.

In the traditional mystery, murder is committed, and the detective investigates, ferrets out the killer and brings him to justice.

You can see that, at the core, genre novels are very moral books. The moral can be stated in a few words:

- Love conquers all. (romance)
- Adherence to law is the foundation of a civilized society. (western)
- Crime does not pay. (mystery)

Most people feel that these things ought to be true, whether it has been so in their own experience or not.

Because genre novels tap into these universal themes, there is a built-in readership just waiting for them to hit the shelves. Genre readers are loyal and have insatiable appetites. When a genre editor buys a book by a new author, she knows the readers are out there, many of them willing to give a newcomer a try.

Genre novels fulfill reader expectations; that is, the reader knows generally what kind of story he's getting when he chooses a book in a particular genre. Therefore, most novels in a genre have certain things in common, a basic structure which the author appropriates for his story.

This is not to say that "When you've read one, you've read them all." The basic skeleton of a traditional mystery, or whodunit, goes something like this: a murder is committed, the sleuth identifies several suspects, overcomes obstacles as he or she follows various lines of investigation, solves the case, and brings the murderer to justice. Within that framework, there is plenty of room for the writer to give his imagination free rein. In fact, more often than not, the mystery that is somehow different from the majority of mysteries wins the major mystery awards: the Edgar, Anthony, Agatha and Macavity. You will find it instructive to read some of these award winners. (For listings, see appendices.)

If you are embarking on the writing of a mystery novel, there's security in knowing:

1. A readership already exists for the kind of book you want to write.
2. There is a tried-and-true basic structure for you to use in *your* novel.

Both of these are good reasons for writing a mystery.

However, the most important qualification for writing in a particular genre is that the writer loves the genre and, therefore, has read many (usually hundreds) of the books. If that is the case, the fledgling mystery writer has already absorbed much of what makes such a novel work.

Don't choose to write a mystery because you think it'll be easier to sell than a mainstream novel. This is not necessarily true, and it certainly won't be true for you if that is the only reason for your choice.

In the early '80's when the big romance boom hit, I was already in on the ground floor, having moved over from the dying gothic market. I enjoyed reading a good romance, and I enjoyed writing them. Before turning to mysteries, I sold about thirty-five romances.

I knew writers who did not really enjoy reading romances, but wanted to write them because the market was hot. Many of those people were good writers, but they were never able to sell a romance novel. They didn't really buy into the ideal (or fantasy, if you prefer), so somehow their tone wasn't quite right. Two of my writing friends, who tried and failed at romances, have since gone on to become extremely successful authors of multiple mystery series. It is no coincidence that both have read mysteries since their childhood days.

Since I began writing mysteries in the late '80's, I've

met mystery writers all over the country. Almost all of the ones I've asked say that, like me, they have been reading mysteries since they were kids, starting with Nancy Drew and the Hardy Boys, going on to books by Agatha Christie, Josephine Tey, Raymond Chandler, and other classical mystery authors, and finally branching out to explore the various mystery sub-genres. Others may not have discovered mysteries until they were past the Nancy Drew stage, but once they did, they became avid mystery readers.

Often readers find they prefer a certain sub-genre of the mystery, such as the amateur sleuth or the Private Eye novel; consequently, they read more in that sub-genre. And when they become writers, they write that kind of book. As a reader, you may favor a particular sub-genre over others. You are well advised to write what you most often choose to read.

Which brings us to the first question you will have to answer: What kind of mystery will you write?

CHAPTER 1

WHAT KIND
OF MYSTERY?

Mysteries can be categorized into various sub-genres. These categories are not hard and fast, and some mysteries do not fit neatly into any one of them. The categories are used merely as a convenient way of talking about mysteries (or reviewing them, in the case of review publications). Some, like many police procedurals and Private Eye novels, are grittier, harder-edged, even downright gory. Others, like most amateur sleuth novels, are *soft-boiled*, as they say in the trade; that is, they contain less on-stage violence than hard-boiled books.

For our purposes, we will separate mysteries into five categories:

- Police Procedural
- Private Investigator
- Historical
- Professional
- Amateur Sleuth

POLICE PROCEDURAL

These are books in which the every day business of police work plays some part in the story, if only as a credible background. Obviously, to write a police procedural, you must know police procedure. However, you don't have to have personal experience in police work. Police procedure can be learned.

If you are using a real town or city, visit the police station (start with the public information officer). Talk to cops, see what their work place looks like, what's on the bulletin boards, etc. Find out what kind of organizational structure the department uses, the titles of the various divisions and positions within each division, what kind of guns they carry, how they talk to each other. And make copious notes.

Take advantage of the ride-along program, if they have one. A gun safety course would also be helpful. You need to know what it feels like to carry and shoot a gun if your sleuth does. If the department has a citizens' police academy, take the course.

Even if the town in your book is fictitious, getting to know your local cops and their daily routine will give you valuable information and ideas which will add verisimilitude to your book. It will also give you sources to contact when questions concerning police procedure arise as you are writing.

What Kind of Mystery?

Most police departments of any size have a volunteer program. Filing papers or copying files a few hours a month will put you on the inside where you will witness cops "being cops" and gain some knowledge of actual police procedure.

If the police procedural is your preference, you are probably already familiar with Ed McBain's 87th Precinct novels. If you haven't read them, you should. Other good police procedurals are written by Reginald Hill, Peter Robinson, Hugh Holton, Julie Smith, Jill McGown, and Carol O'Connell.

In some mysteries, even though the main character is a cop or sheriff—usually in a small town or rural area—the police procedure is given brief, if any, notice. For example, in my Mitch Bushyhead series, Mitch is chief of police in a small Oklahoma town. Rather than police procedure, the cultural and racial mix of the small town's citizens (traditional Cherokees, assimilated Cherokees, and whites) provides background material. Joan Hess's Maggody series is another example. Arly Hanks is the police chief of Maggody, but police procedure is barely touched upon. Rather, it's Joan's humor and eccentric characters that keep readers coming back book after book. Mysteries such as these are hard to pigeonhole into a particular sub-genre. They are simply traditional mysteries.

PRIVATE INVESTIGATOR

Traditionally, the quintessential American crime novel was the private eye novel. Books by Raymond Chandler, Ross MacDonald and Mickey Spillane paved the way for today's wide variety of P. I. novels. In those classic novels, the hero was a hard-drinking, wenching loner traveling the "mean streets" in search of justice for his clients.

The P. I. novel has come a long way since those days. Today's P. I. is as likely to be female as male. He/she may be single, married, divorced or widowed; may have children; may be gay; is as likely to be a teetotaler as a boozer.

Books by Sue Grafton, Marcia Muller, Phillip Craig, Robert Parker, Sandra West Prowell, Linda Barnes, and Lawrence Block, to name only a few, are good examples of the modern Private Eye novel.

HISTORICAL

In recent years, the "history mystery" has drawn many new readers, largely because there are so many good historical mysteries being written. They take place everywhere from ancient Rome to Medieval England.

In addition to telling a good mystery story, the writer of historicals must have a thorough knowledge of the time and place he chooses to write about. If, as a writer, you are drawn to the historical mystery, you probably already have a strong interest in a specific historical period in a particular part of the world. You've undoubtedly done some reading in your area of interest, and you will have to do more. For the writer of historical novels, research never ends. But as a rule historical writers enjoy research. Often the problem is knowing when to *stop* researching and write the book.

Research can be an excuse to avoid writing. Don't let it happen to you. Once you have a good general knowledge of the time and place you're going to use, start writing your mystery. Inevitably, you will discover there are still many details you don't have at your fingertips but need for your book. If possible, make a note to look them up later and keep on writing until you've finished the first draft.

Another danger for the historical writer is the temptation to put too much research into the book. The writer has spent a lot of time and energy digging out information about his historical period. He finds it fascinating and wants to share it with the reader. This impulse should be quashed. If readers want to delve deeply into history, they'll read a non-fiction history book. Remember, the setting is background and should never overshadow the story.

Excellent historical mysteries are books by Sharan

Newman, Ellis Peters, Anne Perry, Lynda Robinson and Lindsay Davis. There are many others.

PROFESSIONAL

Books in this category feature sleuths who are not strictly law enforcement officers, but their professions put them in frequent contact with crime and criminals. Lawyers and crime reporters are prime examples. Those who criticize amateur sleuth novels (invariably hard-boiled fans) say they're not realistic. If that is a problem for you, the difficulty may be overcome by choosing a profession that is more likely to put your sleuth in the way of crime. Good examples of writers (and the professions of their sleuths) in this sub-genre include: Edna Buchanan (crime reporter), William Bernhardt (lawyer), Margaret Maron (judge), Nevada Barr (park ranger), and Abigail Padgett (child abuse investigator).

My Molly Bearpaw series is another example. Molly is employed as an investigator by the Cherokee Nation of Oklahoma. In practice, she is called in when an enrolled Cherokee is involved in a criminal case, either as victim or suspect. She works with whatever law enforcement agency has jurisdiction.

If this sub-genre appeals to you, there are many good books to study, including those by the authors mentioned above.

What Kind of Mystery?

AMATEUR SLEUTH

Agatha Christie's Miss Marple novels are classic examples of this sub-genre. The sleuth can work in almost any job you can imagine—janitor, homemaker, librarian, bookstore owner, teacher, gas meter reader, minister, etc. In my Iris House series, amateur sleuth Tess Darcy owns a bed-and-breakfast inn.

Fans of amateur sleuth novels (sometimes called cozies) have no problem at all with the fact that, in reality, a librarian or a teacher is never likely to stumble over a dead body in an entire lifetime, much less one every few months. They are willing to suspend their disbelief on that point because they love the books so much.

The setting in the amateur sleuth novel is usually self-contained, somewhat insulated, sometimes even isolated—an island, a small town or village, a college campus, a museum. It has been said, in fact, that the setting is so important it's practically another character. Part of the charm of these books is the writer's ability to create a "little world" for readers who enjoy visiting it again and again.

There are many examples of amateur sleuth novels in bookstores. Some of my favorite authors are Carolyn Hart, Joan Hess, Earlene Fowler, Nancy Pickard, Kathy Hogan Trochek, Susan Rogers Cooper, Susan Wittig Albert, David Handler, and Jeff Abbott.

SUSPENSE

In addition to the traditional mysteries discussed above, suspense books and thrillers are sometimes referred to as mysteries. While many thrillers and suspense novels contain murders, they are different from traditional mysteries in several ways. An obvious one is that they are almost always longer. Rarely does a traditional mystery contain more than 80,000-85,000 words, and many are shorter than that. Suspense novels and thrillers are usually at least 100,000 words in length, and some are longer. In addition, they are not necessarily whodunits. Sometimes the reader knows who the bad guy is from the start—the question is not, Who is the murderer? but Will the hero catch the villain before he sets off the bomb or kidnaps the children or stalks and kills another viction or (you fill in the blank)?

It is often difficult to draw the line between the thriller and the suspense novel, and I won't even try. In fact, all these books are suspense novels in the broadest sense. (Sometimes you will even hear a book described as a "suspense thriller.") A few popular suspense authors are David Lindsey, Tami Hoag, Mary Higgins Clark, Richard North Patterson, and Barbara Michaels. While the techniques in this book can easily be adapted to a suspense novel, "mystery" for our purposes means a traditional mystery or whodunit.

CHAPTER 2

THE BIG PICTURE

Before we get to the various techniques you will need to master in writing your novel, let's look at mystery writing in general—things to avoid and guidelines to be followed (or at least carefully considered before being discarded).

TEN COMMON MISTAKES OF BEGINNING MYSTERY WRITERS

1. The story does not grab the reader's attention on the first page. Try to start with a character engaged in an action that arouses the reader's curiosity. Never start with a dream or a flashback.

2. The story starts too soon (often the cause of mistake #1). The reader has to become acquainted with a

character by seeing him in action before he cares about all the background (what brought the character to that point) which beginning writers often think they have to include in the opening pages.

3. The author does not use vivid nouns and verbs, and may try to compensate by using too many adjectives and adverbs.

4. The reader can't "see" the story happening because the author has not used significant details. Instead of showing the reader, he tells him.

5. The story contains too much narrative summary and not enough fully developed scenes. All the important action in the story should be told in scenes (moment by moment) in order for the reader to "experience" it.

6. The story does not contain enough conflict. The next time you're reading a book that drags in places and makes you want to skip ahead to the next section or chapter, stop and ask yourself why. Usually it's because there isn't sufficient conflict to hold your attention. Lack of conflict may be due to mistake #5—too much narration. Remember, fiction is conflict.

7. The author has not made clear the characters' motivations; therefore their actions don't seem credible.

8. There are too many flashbacks. Flashbacks can stop the current action and lose the reader's attention. Avoid them whenever possible.

9. The author does not understand viewpoint and, therefore, the reader is jarred out of the story world.

10. The author does not understand that fictional dialogue is not real-life talk.

TWENTY GUIDELINES FOR BEGINNING MYSTERY WRITERS

1. The mystery is plot-driven, but the characters drive the plot. This is not a contradiction; it merely means that the characters and their motivations should be developed first, and the plot should grow out of that. As we discuss writing techniques, we'll deal with characterization before plot because the best books grow out of character. But the point here is that mystery readers expect a real story (plot) with a beginning, middle, end and a satisfying resolution.

2. Well-developed characters are not stereotypes, neither all bad nor all good. The hero has flaws, and the villain has a redeeming character trait or two.

17

3. There must be at least one murder. You could probably find a book that breaks this rule, but generally, if there's no murder, readers don't come away feeling they've read a real mystery.

4. Some violence is required, but the more soft-boiled your story, the more violence will occur off-stage. The violence should not be gratuitous; it should advance the story line.

5. The hero/heroine cannot be the murderer. Again, you may find a book that breaks this rule, but don't try it unless you are well established as a mystery writer. The reader identifies with the hero and feels betrayed when the person he trusted turns out to be the killer. Also, readers (and editors) think in terms of series, and you'd have a real problem doing a series if in the first book the detective is the culprit.

6. The murderer should appear early. He should at least be mentioned by the end of the third chapter and should appear in one or more scenes in the first quarter of the novel. A traditional mystery must play fair with the reader. One reason the reader is reading a mystery is to try to solve the puzzle before the detective does. He can't do that if the writer has cheated by keeping the killer under

wraps until late in the book.

7. Authenticity is required. Don't irritate a reader who knows more about a subject than you do. For example, if your setting is an actual town, be sure you're using the right streets or subway lines. Get your gun facts and police procedure straight. When you're uncertain about details, do your research and/or consult an expert.

8. Keep chapters short, less than twenty pages as a general rule. Short chapters add to a feeling of a quick pace.

9. Give your detective a distinctive trait, hobby or characteristic gesture or attitude. (For instance, Molly Bearpaw keeps a supply of Snickers candy bars handy. That's her comfort food.)

10. Introduce the dectective early—in the first chapter, if possible.

11. Give the detective a sound motive for becoming involved in the investigation. Even if it's his job, you can make his motivation even stronger by adding a personal reason, too. Amateur sleuths, especially, need this personal reason.

12. Try to make the method of murder or the way the body is found unique and attention-getting.

13. Introduce at least one potential suspect by the end of the second chapter.

14. Introduce a second suspect (or more) by the end of the third chapter. In all you should introduce 4 or 5 suspects in the first quarter of the book.

15. Provide legitimate clues to the killer's identity.

16. The detective should gain some piece of data from every interview and avenue of investigation, even if he is not aware, at the time, which piece of data is relevant.

17. The detective should exhaust one avenue of investigation after another, as the book progresses, until it seems impossible to solve the case.

18. The detective's realization of the killer's identity should come from an accumulation of information and events which he has been sifting through in his mind all along—but which he has been unable to interpret thus far because of a missing but vital clue that he finally uncovers or that he has overlooked because of some preconception

or character flaw of his own. Never drop the solution in the detective's lap through a twist of fate or stupid mistake made by an otherwise clever killer. The detective should solve the puzzle through his own efforts and wit.

19. Neither an act of God nor coincidence should be used to get your hero/heroine out of trouble.

20. Reveal the killer's identity as close to the end of the book as possible. Try to do it in an action scene.

CHAPTER 3

TITLES

In my mystery writing classes and workshops, I've discovered that many beginning writers don't know what makes a good title. Often titles chosen by students have no meaning for the reader, or give no indication that the book is a mystery. Sometimes the author feels he can overcome this by adding a foreword to explain the title. If you have to resort to a foreword or author's note to explain the title of your mystery novel, perhaps you should rethink your choice.

Your title is the first thing a browsing reader sees. If it doesn't intrigue him, he's likely to pass over your book for somebody else's without even reading the cover blurb.

Many good mystery titles have "death," "murder," or "killing" in them. (*Death on the Drunkard's Path, Mint Julep Murder, The Killing of Monday Brown*).

On the next page is a list of some of the mysteries in my own personal library.

Prayers for the Dead by Faye Kellerman
Thyme of Death by Susan Wittig Albert
No Sign of Murder by Alan Russell
A Killing in Quail County by Jameson Cole
Written in Blood by Caroline Graham
Innocent Graves by Peter Robinson
Three to Get Deadly by Janet Evanovich
Murder on the Iditarod Trail by Sue Henry
Death Down Home by Eve K. Sandstrom
Murder at Moot Point by Marlys Millhiser
Roll Over and Play Dead by Joan Hess
Dying for Chocolate by Diane Mott Davidson

There is little doubt as to what kind of books these are.

Some mysteries have titles that tie the series together—Sue Grafton's alphabet series, for example (*A is for Alibi, B is for Burglar*, etc.). William Bernhardt's series titles all have "justice" in them (*Primary Justice, Blind Justice, Perfect Justice*, etc.). Since quilts figure in Earlene Fowler's Benni Harper series, the titles are names of quilt patterns: *Fools' Puzzle, Irish Chain, Kansas Troubles, Goose in the Pond.*

Titles in Jill Churchill's popular amateur sleuth series are familiar phrases or clichés with a catchy change in one of the words that makes the reader look twice and then smile.

(*Grime and Punishment, A Quiche Before Dying, Silence of the Hams*) I used a similar technique for the title of my Iris House Christmas mystery, *The Last Noel*.

Sometimes familiar phrases can be used unchanged. Lawrence Block's mystery *A Stab in the Dark* is a good example. Other examples are Janet Evanovich's *One for the Money*, Susan Rogers Cooper's *Home Again, Home Again* and Margaret Maron's *Up Jumps the Devil*.

I recommend coming up with your title before you write the book, or at least in the early stages of writing. If the title is a good one, it will communicate the essence of your book and give you a focus as you write.

Titles are important! Choose yours carefully.

CHAPTER 4

CHARACTERIZATION

Published mystery writers will tell you that, when readers comment on their books, they almost always mention the characters. Before my fourth Mitch Bushyhead book, *The Fire Carrier*, came out and answered the question, a frequent query from readers was "Are Mitch and Lisa going to get married?" I get simiilar questions about my other series sleuths, Molly Bearpaw and Tess Darcy, both of whom have had long-term love relationships.

Rarely does a reader comment on things like plot or description. This was surprising to me at first, but then I realized that the readers were actually paying me a compliment. My series characters are real to them, and they care about what might happen in their futures.

Chances are you remember the characters in your favorite books much more clearly than the plots. You probably remember a character you lived with for several days or weeks; perhaps you didn't want the book to end. Creating "real," credible characters is the most important part of writing a novel. Characters make your story. If they come alive, what they do *becomes* the story. When you realize that, you can stop obsessing so much about plot.

When a writer has to write a plot synopsis before he writes the book (usually because it's stipulated in his publishing contract as a prerequisite to getting advance money released), the book he writes later will likely turn out considerably different from the way the writer conceived it when he wrote the synopsis. Fortunately editors understand this and they don't care, as long as they are satisfied with the completed manuscript. This is not to say that plot is unimportant, but that's a subject for a later chapter.

Editors will tell you that what they hope for when they pick up a manuscript is to be swept up as quickly as possible into the life of a character so interesting that they have to keep reading to find out what happens to him. I've heard more than one editor say, "I'll buy a book with a so-so plot if the characters are wonderful."

Sometimes a competent writer can write an action-packed beginning, get all his facts straight, write good description, and devise a good story line but somehow the reader doesn't connect to the story because he doesn't come to know and care about the characters.

In real life, terrible things happen to people all the time, but we don't care nearly as much when something bad (or good, for that matter) happens to a stranger as we would if the same thing happened to somebody close to us. This is equally true in fiction. The events of a story do not seriously affect our emotions unless we know the characters—and the goal of fiction is to affect our emotions.

You must connect emotionally with a wide variety of readers. You do that by learning the art of characterization, adding details and depth until you have created a character whom your readers may come to know as well as they know their closest friends. To create this "magic" you must first know your characters well yourself. If you know your characters, they'll come into the story acting "in character"—being themselves. Obviously, they can't do that if *you* don't know them first.

Characterization isn't easy, but it is the most important technique in the writing of memorable fiction.

Some writers start by writing a character sketch. The sketch includes the character's name, sex, age, physical description, education, vocation/occupation, social status and income, marital status, family/ethnicity, diction/accent, relationships (personal and professional), brief descriptions of places where the character spends time (home, office, car, etc.), recreation/hobbies, religion (ethics/morals), obsessions, sexual history, ambitions, superstitions, fears, character flaws, pets, taste in books, music, food, etc. You can add to the list if you want.

Personally I have a difficult time writing a very detailed character sketch before I'm well into the book. Usually all I have when I start to write Chapter One is a brief description of each character (aside from my main character, whom I know because I've gotten well acquainted with him/her in previous books) and his relationships to the other characters. The best way for me to get to know my characters is to put them into scenes and conflict situations and let them act and react. This means that I usually have to go back and rewrite the early chapters in the book, after I'm well along, because I've come to know the characters better and I can sharpen their actions and speech, making them more "in character."

I admit this is not the most efficient way to work. If you can get to know your characters by first writing a detailed character sketch of each one, then do so. And you won't know until you try it. You have to find out what works for you.

It is vital that you know your characters' motivations and that you convey those motivations to the reader. You should know why a character does whatever he does in the story. What's his motivation? Why is Sue spreading lies about her co-worker? Why is Harry trying to pick a fight with John? Why does Sally stay in a relationship that depresses her? Why did Michael kill Hortense? (Because she wanted a divorce. Because she was blackmailing him. Because he molested her daughter and she was going to to the police. Because she had an affair with his best friend. The possibilities are virtually endless.)

Your characters' motivations dictate the story line. If readers find something in your story hard to believe, chances are it's because you either haven't given the characters strong enough motivations or you've failed to get the motivations across to the reader. You can make anything believable if it's properly motivated.

Beginning writers sometimes find it difficult to give the hero strong enough motivations, and the hero comes off as weak-willed and lacking in drive. Sometimes the writer avoids putting the hero in strong conflict situations because he identifies with the hero too much. This makes for a boring story.

Good heroes and heroines are not passive; they're active, they take charge, they strive to attain their goals. When they get knocked down, they get up and try again. To add conflict to your story as you go from one scene to the next, ask yourself, "What's the worst thing that could happen now?" Conflict keeps the reader reading.

To be believable rather than stereotypical, the

hero/heroine should have some paradox in his charaacter; that is, some character trait that surprises the reader because he doesn't expect it from that type of character—for example, a hard-bitten homicide detective who writes poetry, or an always elegantly groomed and dressed society woman who vacations at archeological digs where she does hard, dirty manual labor. A good hero also has a character flaw or two—for example, your detective may have grown up hating and fearing his father's hair-trigger temper, but he fails to recognize the same tendency in himself.

As for the villain, he must be as strong-willed as the hero, as determined to achieve his ends. In a mystery, the villain will kill to get what he wants and often he will murder again to keep from being exposed. But, just as the hero is not completely heroic in all aspects of his character, the villain is not totally evil, either. For instance, a murderer might kill without remorse and refuse to take a hint of an insult from anybody, except his mother who is the only person in the world he truly loves. She may order him around and verbally abuse him without his so much as raising his voice to her. That one trait which goes against the stereotype will make him seem more human to the reader. And many times it's that chink in his armor that gets him caught in the end.

Delete long physical descriptions of your characters.

Characterization

Substitute images conveyed in precise vivid language that lets the reader see the character, as three or four brush strokes can evoke a bird or a flower. A good writer can describe a character with a few well-chosen words.

In *By Evil Means*, Sandra West Prowell describes an instructor at the FBI firing range as "a big guy with no neck and a heart of gold."

Reginald Hill, in *Bones and Silence*, describes a bumbling constable as "one of Mid-Yorkshire's most reliable men. He always got it wrong."

In *A Long Line of Dead Men*, Lawrence Block gives us a clear picture of an elderly man with white hair, beaked nose, and pale blue eyes magnified by thick glasses, when he compares him to a figure carved on the prow of a Viking ship. "Some great idealized bird of prey, scanning the horizon, seeing for miles and miles, for years and years."

When revising, pay particular attention to physical descriptions. Keep them brief, but make them fresh and vivid. Giving the reader a mental picture is far more effective than a long laundry list of physical characteristics.

The best way to characterize, however, is through actions. If you know your character well, he'll act "in character"—be himself, thus conveying to the reader what kind of person he is. Describing an action, *showing* the reader, is far more effective than simply telling him in a paragraph of narrative.

Don't put down the first thing that comes to mind. "Susan was fifty pounds overweight." That's the easy way, the lazy way. Instead, describe an action: "Susan always wore black mumus to hide her excess weight." Now you've let the reader *see* Susan. You've shown him, rather than told him.

Here's how I introduced one of the characters in my Iris House mystery *Sew Deadly* (published by Avon Books, copyright 1998 by Jean Hager):

> "I'm going to kill her!" Ross Dellin shouted as he barrelled into the room. Three women who stood in the doorway scattered like trespassing children fleeing a charging bull.
> Regulars at the senior citizens' center were used to Ross's bovine-like method of locomotion, head thrust forward as though he were looking for something to butt out of his way, bushy white eyebrows bristling. But murder threats were a bit over the top, even for Ross.

You learn a lot about Ross from those four sentences. He's a senior citizen, he's aggressive, loud and blustery. And *showing* Ross in action communicates much more effectively than just telling the reader what he's like.

Here's a lengthier example, this one from my Iris House mystery *Dead and Buried* (Avon Books, 00-380-77210-8, copyright 1995 by Jean Hager). At the beginning of Chapter One, I introduce literary agent Rita De'Lane, a tense, colorful and impatient woman who's about to lose her best-selling author to another agency and fears she could lose her job because of it. She is determined not to let that happen.

Rita De'Lane's glittering, sienna-nailed finger stabbed out the airline's number on the touch tone dial. Clutching the receiver to her ear, she paced across her apartment as far as the cord would stretch, spun around on one heel, and paced back again. If she had been a cartoon, smoke would have been curling from her ears. As it was, she was angry enough to tear the phone from the wall. But that would be like getting mad at the cat and kicking the dog. And then she'd have to go out and use a pay phone.

She muttered an oath. *Blasted voice mail.* You could never get hold of a real person these days without first listening to this garbage and punching more buttons. She gave it ten years before every business in the city was run totally by computers. Human beings would be obsolete.

At the prompting of the recorded message, she hissed another purple curse and jabbed "2."

When a ticket agent finally answered, she barked, "So pleased you could bother with little old me."

"Ma'am?"

"Did you enjoy your lunch?"

"Pardon me?"

"Never mind." The jerk didn't even recognize sarcasm when he heard it. "How soon can you get me to Victoria Springs, Missouri?"

"Say again, ma'am."

"VICTORIA SPRINGS, MISSOURI!" she bellowed. "I have to get there right away. This is an emergency."

"We don't fly into Victoria Springs, ma'am."

Great. It figured.

"What's the nearest city?" the agent asked.

"How the hell should I know! Look it up!"

"One moment, please."

Rita tapped her foot furiously. Leave it to Francine, Rita's temperamental-writer client, to hole up in the boondocks where there wasn't even an airport. Well, it would take more brainpower than Francine Alexander possessed to outwit Rita De'Lane.

In a short scene, the reader gets a pretty good idea what kind of person Rita is. As the story progresses, I flesh out Rita's character. For one thing, her appearance is outlandish by Victoria Springs standards. She wears her hair in a man-like burr cut and dresses in eye-popping garbs, from combat boots to a bustier.

Contrast is another good technique of characterization. Characters who are opposites in many areas play off each other in ways that emphasize their differences, thus helping to characterize both.

Characterization

In Shari Geller's *Fatal Convictions*, the two police partners could hardly be more different. Randazzo is a young, ambitious female detective who is striving to excel in a world historically reserved for men. She has a new husband and an unending drive to succeed. What she lacks in experience, she compensates for with painstaking attention to detail. She is determined to solve the case, even at the risk of making a mistake. By contrast, Larson, her partner, is a man who has long since burned out, his enthusiasm dulled by twenty years on the force and a succession of rookie partners. He's had two failed marriages, which have left him jaded and emotionally numb.

Opposites may attract, but they also clash, as is often the case in *Fatal Convictions*. In addition to the conflicts inherent in their characters, conflict between the two detectives is heightened when Larson falls for the prime suspect in the case.

Look at the secondary characters in your novel, particularly your detective's sidekick (partner, friend, confidant). Can you deepen your characterizations by making the sidekick the opposite of the sleuth? This will not only help flesh out the character of both, but it will give you many opportunities for conflict between the two.

Other characterization techniques include comparison, physical traits and behavior, and exaggeration.

Saying "Jeffrey could have stood flat-footed and

looked eye to eye with Michael Jordan" gets the point across with a comparison without the author telling the reader that Jeffrey is very tall.

"I closed my eyes and let my partner whirl me around the dance floor. He made me feel like Ginger Rogers." communicates to the reader that the partner is a good dancer without the writer actually making that statement.

Instead of saying that a person is shy and self-conscious, it's more effective to report a characteristic action. "I wanted her to meet my gaze, but she was examining her skirt for invisible stains."

When one character tells another something that makes him angry, instead of simply stating the fact, show the reader by showing a characteristic reaction. "George gaped at me as I relayed the message. Then he snatched the dictionary from the desk and threw it against the wall."

Occasionally exaggeration communicates what you want to say better than a direct statement. "Toni was so thin that when she turned sideways, she disappeared."

You may find it helpful to keep colored markers handy when you're reading. Highlight effective passages of characterization. Pay particular attention to those that give you a visual image. Later, when you want to characterize somebody in your book, glance through the novels you've marked and study the high-lighted passages—not to copy them, but to stimulate your imagination.

CHAPTER **5**

DIALOGUE

Dialogue, along with characteristic actions, is at the top of the list of effective methods of characterization. One of the problems in unpublished writers' fiction is often related to dialogue. All the characters speak alike. Unless the writer tells you who's speaking, you can't tell. You should be able to identify the speaker from what the character says or how he says it. Each character's dialogue should be consistent with who he is.

Sometimes beginning writers don't understand that fictional dialogue is not like real life conversation.

Real life talk is full of repetitions:

"Why are you doing that?"

"What did you say?"

"Why are you doing that?"

"Oh. That's what I thought you said."

This conversation is going nowhere. Real life conversation is full of repetition, but it doesn't belong in dialogue.

Real life conversation is full of meaningless words and phrases:

"What did Janey tell you?"

"Well, er—uh, let me see. She was kind of tired, you know. I can't remember her exact words. It was like—well, you know, like she didn't want to talk."

Cut out those meaningless words and phrases, unless you are using a particular one as a character tag.

Real life conversation is often mundane and pointless.

"How are you?"

"I'm fine. How are you?"

"Fine."

This is pointless talk. It doesn't belong in fictional dialogue.

When writing dialogue, or checking it on revision, ask yourself the following questions:

1. Does this section of dialogue have a purpose? (All dialogue should have a purpose; it should advance the story.)

2. Does this exchange create or heighten a conflict?

3. Does this exchange create tension?

4. Does this exchange arouse readers' curiosity?

5. Is this exchange going anywhere? (i.e., does it build to a climax, an unexpected turn of events, or provide necessary information?)

6. Is each character's dialogue consistent with who that character is? (His background, education, traits, etc.)

Dialogue is not speech-making. Many beginning writers write sections of dialogue that go on too long and confuse readers by containing several thoughts thrown together in a single block. Dialogue should be short and crisp, not necessarily grammatically correct or in complete sentences. It should reflect the way the character actually talks.

Remember, too, that "said" is a perfectly good word. Don't overuse an array of substitutes; using too many "said" synonyms tends to irritate the reader. If only two characters are talking, you won't even have to use "said" more than a couple of times. If you don't overuse "said" synonyms, when you *do* need one for effect, because the character *did* "shriek" or "grumble," etc., it will be more convincing.

Often replacing "said" or a "said" substitute with an action is an effective way of identifying the speaker.

Joyce walked to the window and pushed back the curtain. "He didn't come home last night."

Readers like dialogue because it moves the story along at a good clip. When a story seems to drag, they'll skip ahead to the next section of dialogue. Try reading your dialogue into a tape recorder and playing it back. Often you will hear repetitions, useless words and phrases, and uncharacteristic talk that got by you when you merely read the words silently from a manuscript or computer screen. Reading dialogue to a friend who's a good critic can also be helpful. When reading somebody else's book, notice how professional writers use dialogue to characterize. Here's the opening of *Fade Away* by Edgar and Anthony Award-winning author Harlan Coben:

"Just behave."

"Me?" Myron said. "I'm always a delight."

Myron Bolitar was being led through the corridor of the darkened Meadowlands Arena by Calvin Johnson, the New Jersey Dragons new general manager. Their dress shoes clacked sharply against the tile and echoed through empty Harry M. Stevens food stands, Carvel Ice Cream carts, pretzel vendors, souvenir booths. The smell of sporting-event hot dogs—that sort of rubbery, chemically, yet nostalgically delicious aroma—wafted from the walls. The stillness of the place consumed them; there is nothing more hollow and lifeless than an empty sports arena.

Calvin Johnson stopped in front of a door leading to a luxury box. "This may all seem a bit strange," he said. "Just go with the flow, okay?"

"Okay."

Calvin reached for the knob and took a deep breath. "Clip Arnstein, the owner of the Dragons, is in there waiting for us."

"And yet I'm not trembling," Myron said.

Calvin Johnson shook his head. "Just don't be an ass."

Myron pointed to his chest. "I wore a tie and everything."
(Reprinted by permission of Dell Publishing from *Fade Away*, 95-1090-01 by Harlan Coben. Copyright 1996 by Harlan Coben.)

Even if this were the first Myron Bolitar mystery you'd read, already in the first few lines of the book, you begin to get a feel for what kind of character sports agent Myron Bolitar is: wise-cracking, sardonic, not overly impressed by the movers and shakers in the sports world.

Now, read the following exchange from Carolyn Hart's *A Little Class on Murder* and see what you can learn about amateur sleuth Annie's mother-in-law, Laurel:

"A class on the greatest ladies of the mystery? On Mary Roberts Rinehart?" The rising note of excitement in Laurel's husky voice was the first indication to Max Darling that his idle chatter, his well-meant, *innocuous* report of his and Annie's doings, was of altogether too much interest to his mother. When Laurel got that particular tone in her voice, that vibrato—
Max stiffened. Which wasn't easy when lying almost horizontal in the soft leather embrace of his reclining desk chair. Not even the soothing warmth of the heater assuaged the sudden chill enveloping his mind.
"I'll write you all about it, Laurel. I'll keep you informed. I'll send you the books on her reading list. Of course, Annie's hoping that

no one she knows enrolls. Her first time to teach, you know."

"My dear child, Annie must be *confident.* Maxwell, we must *encourage* Annie."

"That's just it," he said heartily. "We'll be behind the scenes. *Behind the scenes,* Mother."

"A noble thought, Maxwell dear. You do phrase things so beautifully. Just like Rasheesh."

Max pursed his lips and frowned.

Light laughter, reminiscent of leprechauns in the twilight. "My newest link to the Other Side, my dear."

(Reprinted by permission of Doubleday from *A Little Class on Murder,* 99-0004-01, by Carolyn G. Hart. Copyright 1989 by Carolyn G. Hart.)

Can you see Laurel staying out of Annie's first attempt at teaching? Not on your life. Laurel is always sure she knows what's best for those close to her, better than they know themselves. From Annie's and Max's viewpoints, she's an interfering mother-in-law; in Laurel's mind, she's merely trying to help. Even from this short passage, you already suspect that stopping Laurel doing anything she's set her mind to do is virtually impossible. This passage also hints at another of Laurel's characteristics: she frequently dabbles in "new interests." (Here it's her "link to the Other Side.")

By the time you've finished your first draft, you've lived with your characters for months and know them well.

Dialogue

As you go back through to rewrite and revise, pay particular attention to sharpening the dialogue in ways that make it reflect the character of each speaker.

CHAPTER **6**

VIEWPOINT

If I had to choose one single reason why so many first novelists fail to get published, it's that they don't understand viewpoint.

Try this exercise. Look around you. Are you inside a house—in the kitchen, the living room, a bedroom? Are you outside, in the back yard, on the front porch? Suppose you're outside in the back yard. What do you see? Standing in the northwest corner of my back yard, I see the back of my stone house on the east, dining room and living room windows, a patio door, a wood deck with a white wrought iron table and chairs, a gas grill; on the west edge of the yard is a four-foot high retaining wall made of railroad ties. This is what I see from my viewpoint. If I were writing from the viewpoint of a character standing in my back yard, I would not describe the front yard or a room inside the house because the character would not be seeing that.

The reader identifies with the viewpoint character. He sees, hears, tastes, smells, feels, thinks what that character sees, hears, tastes, smells, feels, thinks. He's inside that character's head. In his imagination, he *becomes* that character. This gives him a focus for experiencing the story.

For the viewpoint character, choose the central character, the one most involved in the action, whose struggle to reach his goal drives the story. In most traditional mysteries, this is the sleuth.

What are the various viewpoint options? Give these some thought before you choose the one you'll use in your story.

FIRST PERSON ("I said," "I did.")

The first person is used in various kinds of novels, including mysteries. In first person novels, the viewpoint is that of the narrator (the "I" character). In mysteries, that's usually the sleuth.

<u>Advantages of First Person Viewpoint:</u>

1. It's more intimate than third person, and therefore draws the reader into the story immediately.

2. It's credible. When the story is told in the first person, the effect is of the narrator telling what happened

to him as it happened. It is an eye-witness account. When a character speaks directly to you, it's easier to believe what he's saying.

3. It's easier to give your narrator a distinctive voice when you're using the "I" viewpoint.

Disadvantages of the First Person Viewpoint:

1. You are limited to a single viewpoint, that of the narrator. The reader can only be told what happens to the viewpoint character (what he sees, hears, thinks, etc.). He either has to be present in every scene or another character has to tell him what happened. You must always guard against telling the reader something that sounds like the author talking, rather than the character.

2. If the sleuth is present in every scene, you can lose some suspense.

3. It's harder to hide pertinent information from the reader without making him feel cheated when he reaches the end of the story and discovers the sleuth held out on him.

4. It's harder to let the reader know what the viewpoint character looks like. It's become trite to have

the character look at his reflection in a mirror and describe what he sees, so you have to come up with a fresher method. For example, another character might say, "I'd give anything for hair like yours. It's rare to see that deep red color."

5. It's easier for the writer to ramble in the "I" viewpoint and include things that serve no purpose in the story being told.

6. The writer must be careful not to let the viewpoint character seem immodest. Lines like "I always won the beauty pageants when I was in college" sound like bragging and make the reader dislike the character.

THIRD PERSON ("He/she said," "He/she did.")
Third person is the most frequent choice for novelists, including mystery writers. In third person, the writer can choose to limit the viewpoint to that of the main character (as in the first person viewpoint). More often, he'll use multiple viewpoints, getting into several characters' heads during the course of the story. If you choose multiple viewpoints, use only one viewpoint at a time. It's confusing to the reader to have to "jump heads" from one sentence to the next.

Switch viewpoints when it will add to the reader's

understanding and enjoyment of the story, but only at the beginning of a new chapter—or at least a new scene. And establish immediately whose viewpoint is being used in that chapter or scene.

I use multiple third person viewpoint because it gives my books greater perspective. Getting in the heads of characters other than the lead character gives me leeway to develop secondary characters more fully and communicate more emotion to the reader.

Switching viewpoints provides relief and variety for the reader and helps sustain reader interest. It can also add to the reader's suspense. For example, if you leave one character in a difficult situation at the end of a chapter and go to another viewpoint character in the next chapter, the reader's suspense over what happened to the first character is heightened.

If you decide to use multiple viewpoints, however, remember that the majority of the story should still be told from the lead character's viewpoint.

The main disadvantage of the third person viewpoint is that you lose some of the immediacy of first person. I have known writers who write their novels in first person in order to capture that immediacy, then change to third person when they rewrite.

I chose third person multiple viewpoint for all three of my mystery series because I believe its advantages outweigh its disadvantages.

OMNISCIENT VIEWPOINT

With the omniscient viewpoint, the narrator is God-like. He can get into any character's head at any time; he can also tell the reader things that none of the characters knows. It is very difficult to employ this viewpoint well, and it is rarely used today.

Even well-used, the omniscient viewpoint is not as credible as either of the more commonly used viewpoints because it is foreign to the reader's experience. Since the reader experiences real life from only one viewpoint, his own, it is easy for him to identify with one viewpoint character at a time. He can't identify with the omniscient viewpoint because, consciously or unconsciously, he finds it unbelievable. In his own life, he can't be in two places at the same time, or be aware of things that are outside his own experience and knowledge. The author who chooses the omniscient viewpoint puts the reader at a distance from the story. Today's fiction reader wants immediacy, not distance.

Occasionally, the omniscient viewpoint can be used to good effect, if it is used very sparingly, for example to set a scene at the beginning of a chapter I made use of it at the beginning of my Molly Bearpaw mystery, *The Redbird's Cry*:

Autumn in northeast Oklahoma is like an indolent beauty who's all dressed up with no place to go. She often dawdles through September, October, November, and sometimes lags right on through Christmas. Leaves drooping in the humid summer heat, revive and paint the countryside crimson and orange and yellow. In Cherokee County, where small towns nestle in valleys surrounded by wooded Ozark foothills, the trees flaunt themselves in a grand, flamboyant display. Autumn's glory reaches its zenith in October, the season the ancient Cherokees called *Dun'nadee'*, the harvest moon. Days may be warm, but by then the nights have turned chilly and invigorating.

On such a mid-October night, at twenty-five minutes after midnight, a car traveling south from Tahlequah turned off Highway 62 into the Cherokee tribal complex. (*The Redbird's Cry*, Mysterious Press, 09-89296-494-4, copyright 1994 by Jean Hager)

In this example, I set the scene, then got into a character's viewpoint and stayed there until the scene ended, when I switched to another character. The majority of the novel is told from Molly's viewpoint.

Omniscient viewpoint can be used if that is the only way to convey certain information. Even then, use it in small doses. Unless you are very sure you know what you are doing, don't try to use the omniscient viewpoint at all.

SECOND PERSON ("you say," "you do")

In the second person viewpoint, the narrator speaks using "you" instead of "I" or "he/she." For example: "You walk out of your house one day, on the way to work, minding your own business, and you see the most beautiful woman in the world. She smiles. You smile back." And so on.

This viewpoint can irritate some readers and its use is even rarer than the omniscient viewpoint.

POINTS TO REMEMBER ABOUT VIEWPOINT

1 Use only one viewpoint at a time.

2. Switch viewpoints only at the beginning of a new chapter—or at least a new scene.

3. Establish immediately the identity of the viewpoint character.

4. Don't inadvertently step out of viewpoint. Example: "Alice ran down the hall and threw open the front door. She was going to be late for work. Again. The rush of wind made her cheeks turn red and her brown eyes water." (This starts in Alice's viewpoint, but the writer steps out of that viewpoint when he describes her red cheeks and brown eyes. Since Alice isn't looking in a mirror, she can't see her cheeks and eyes.)

5. If you are using third person and having trouble staying in viewpoint, try writing the sections that are

giving you a problem in first person. That often makes it easier to see failures in viewpoint.

6. Avoid second person and, except for an occasional brief passage to set a scene, avoid the omniscient viewpoint.

7. Whatever your viewpoint, write in the past tense. Present tense is extremely difficult to maintain effectively, and it tends to put the reader off.

CHAPTER 7

SETTING/DESCRIPTION

With the rise of the "regional mystery" in the past few years, setting has become an important part of most mystery novels. The reader likes to feel he's visited a real place, whether your setting is actual or fictitious. You give him that feeling through effective use of sense impressions in describing your setting. Do this and you make your setting real for the reader.

Be aware of whose viewpoint you're in when you describe something. A young man who is heartbroken over being jilted by his fiancée will see a scene differently than a boy of ten who's having a wonderful time vacationing with his family. The broken-hearted young man might look at the ocean and see a vast, lonely emptiness. He might even wonder how it would feel to walk out into the water until the waves cover his head. The ten-year-old boy might look at the same ocean from the same vantage point and imagine the exhilaration of riding the waves on a surfboard.

The following passage from Sharyn McCrumb's New York Times Best Seller *She Walks These Hills* is in the viewpoint of a man in a prison cell.

Hiram Sorley's feet itched, and he knew it was a sign. The doctor at the prison infirmary might call it dry skin from sweaty three-day socks or athlete's foot from the dank concrete shower room, but Hiram knew better. He had seen the flashes of lightning from the sealed window of his cell: another portent high-lighting the message from the Almighty to him. He'd been getting the signs for days now. The Lord was trying to tell him something, and directly it would all be coming clear.

The window was long and narrow, like a church window, and the glow of the storm through black sheepskin clouds gave it the luminescence of stained glass. He sat down on his bunk beneath the window, with his palm-sized King James Bible cradled in his lap.

(Reprinted by permission of Scribner, a Division of Simon & Schuster, from *She Walks These Hills* by Sharyn McCrumb. Copyright 1994 by Sharyn McCrumb.)

The writer has stayed in-character in this description. Only someone in Hiram Sorley's mental state would consider itching feet and lightning direct messages to him from God, or compare the cell window to a church window.

Instead of stopping your story dead in order to add a few paragraphs of description, try to sprinkle in the description around the action. The following example is from the same book by Sharyn McCrumb. Notice how she gives us a picture of the setting without ever stopping the action.

The woman had been running through the woods a long time. Blood crusted in the briar-cut on her cheek. Her matted hair, a thicket of dry leaves and tangles, hung about a gaunt face, lined with weariness and hunger. A shapeless, dirt-streaked dress that had once been blue gaped over bony wrists and sagged empty at the collarbone. She might have been twenty, but her eyes were old.

She was following the deer track that hugged the ridge above the river, moving silently past dark clumps of rhododendrons, and always watching, looking back across the Tennessee mountains to see that no one followed her, looking down to make sure that the green river still curled around the hollows below. Sometimes she seemed to be no more than a pin oak's shadow, or a trick of light among the leaves at dusk, so colorless and silent was she among the trees. She seemed to hear nothing. She did not appear to feel the scrape of twigs across her face, or the chill of the evening breeze on the mountain. She looked only down and back. Down and back.

(Reprinted by permission of Scribner, a Division of Simon & Schuster, from *She Walks These Hills* by Sharyn McCrumb. Copyright 1994 by Sharyn McCrumb.)

Houses, offices and rooms should reflect the character

of the person who occupies them. It's another way to show the reader what a character is like without telling him directly.

Notice how much you can learn about Orrin Ivory from this description of her front room, from Teri Holbrook's novel *A Far and Deadly Cry*. You also learn something about Gale Grayson, whose living room is compared to Orrin Ivory's.

> This room, like Gale Grayson's front room, was all white. But whereas Mrs. Grayson's was cool with lines and angles, this parlour strangled the air with an overabundance of white lace and flounces. Pleated eyelet draperies with frilly trim puddled around the base of the tall windows, forcing even today's dull light through tiny holes. On sunny days, he imagined the light dotted the white carpet like sunrise rippling on a mouldy lake. (Reprinted by permission of Bantam Books from *A Far and Deadly Cry*, 93-0260-01, by Teri Holbrook. Copyright 1995 by Teri Peitso-Holbrook.)

Don't Leave Out Background or Treat it as Secondary

Exploit your setting, use it to advantage. If you haven't decided on a setting yet, choose a place that lends itself to atmosphere and exploit the locale to the fullest. If you set your book in a real place, choose a place that you know well. If possible, visit it often while you are writing your book. Jot down images and impressions and take plenty of snapshots. These notes and pictures will help you remember the details of the setting when you're back at your desk.

Other points to keep in mind about setting include:

Give the Reader Sense Impressions and Metaphors

Use strong images. Instead of "It had snowed the night before and now it was sleeting," show the bare tree branches mounded with snow. Let the reader experience the numbing of your character's face as he steps outside. Let him hear the crunch as a boot breaks through the crust of snow. Let him see the leaden gray of the sky and feel the sting of sleet driven by gusting winds.

Don't Cut Corners

Visit the location of each scene, get the feel of it, and take notes. If your story takes place in the winter time, it's important to visit the location at that time of year. If you absolutely cannot visit your location, research it thoroughly with books and pictures. Take the extra time and trouble to interview people who've been there. Even if your setting is fictitious, you will find it extremely helpful to use a real town, or house, or police station as a starting point. For example, visit a real police station in a town the

61

approximate size of the town in your book. You will find many details you can use to make your fictitious police station seem authentic.

When I was writing *The Spirit Caller*, which is set in Tahlequah, Oklahoma, I needed to write a scene set in the sheriff's department. Since Tahlequah is more than an hour's drive from my home, I was tempted to wing it. After all, aren't all small town sheriff's departments similar?

But I suppressed the impulse and made the trip, where I was taken on a tour of the sheriff's department by a helpful deputy. I picked up numerous details that I could never have imagined. For instance, a sign in the booking room announced that any prisoner who broke a lightbulb in the jail would be guilty of a felony and would have to either post bond of $1,000 or pay a fine of $100. The deputy explained they'd put the sign up after a couple of prisoners had decided that eating crushed glass was the fastest way out of jail!

Of course, that went in my book. As did the list of "jail rules" and the sign on the inside of the door leading into the foyer, the last thing a deputy saw as he left the sheriff's department. It cautioned, "Don't forget your gun."

Don't Overdo It

A couple of paragraphs of description can go a long way. Slip in nuggets of information—history, economics, etc.—but don't get carried away. When it comes to description, a little does a lot.

Don't Overlook Weather

What's the month, day and year? Is it cold or hot—or somewhere in between. Is it sunny, foggy? Is it raining? Is water running off houses from snow melt? Is the wind blowing? Use the five senses in describing the weather.

CHAPTER 8

OPENINGS

Today's reader is impatient. He's not going to stay with you through a slow opening to get to the good stuff. You have to hook him on the first page. A sure-fire way to do this is to start in the middle of things This is not the place for background information and long descriptions. Instead, show the reader something happening, maybe throw in a few lines of dialogue. Action hooks the reader.

I've heard editors say they can read three paragraphs and know whether the manuscript is something they might be interested in. You may have written a good story, but if you don't grab the editor on the first page, chances are she will read no further. Unfair? Maybe so, but it does no good to bemoan the fact. Just make sure your opening—whether or not it shows a character in action— is so intriguing that the editor *has* to keep reading to find out what happens next.

Here's what editors are looking for in those first three paragraphs:

- A first paragraph that intrigues them, raises their curiosity, draws them into the story, makes them want to find out what happens next. Jodie Larsen says that the editor who bought her first suspense novel, *Deadly Company*, told Jodie's agent that when she read the first sentence, she was pretty sure she was going to buy the book. It read: "Hanna Shore never had a chance." When I read Jodie's book, that sentence hooked me, too. It raised questions. Who's Hanna Shore? Why doesn't she have a chance? What's going to happen to her?

- Good writing. Today's fiction market is very competitive. A manuscript that might have sold several years ago may have no chance now. Good, polished writing could make the difference. I advise my students to get the story down first. Then concentrate on the finer points. Go through the manuscript and throw out all the tired, stale phrases, the clichés like, "She was as flat as a board." or "He looked like something the cat dragged in." Substitute fresh, colorful images to describe character and setting. These won't be the first phrases that occur to you. The clichés will come first;

that's the easy way. But it won't sell. So go through your first draft concentrating on descriptions of characters and setting. Discard the first, even the second and third images that come to mind. Visualize what you're describing. How can you show it to the reader in an original way that will immediately give him a mental picture? Most of us have lazy phrases we tend to use over and over. "He shrugged." "She smiled." "She nodded." Cut them to a bare minimum, and come up with something new. Chances are you've overused adverbs and adjectives. Cut out many of them and substitute strong nouns and verbs. (More on these points in the chapter on revising.)

- A fresh voice is the third thing editors are looking for when they read the first page or two of your manuscript. Harlan Coben has a distinct voice in his Myron Bolitar mysteries. So does Janet Evanovich in her Stephanie Plum books. If you haven't read these authors, do so. But don't try to imitate a favorite author. Write your book in *your* voice.

You will find it helpful to keep a notebook. In the notebook, copy all the good opening lines you find in other people's books. Also, write in your notebook fresh images and vivid descriptions you find in other people's books.

I'm not suggesting here that you lift somebody else's passage, change a few words and stick it in your book. But study the entries in your notebook from time to time, asking yourself, "Why did this opening hook me?" "How did the author give me such a sharp picture of this person or setting?" Your answers will help you improve your own writing.

Keep your notebook with you and concentrate on observing things around you with a writer's eye. Along with passages you've copied from other people's books, add your own images to your notebook. When a place or incident arouses an emotion in you, try to capture that emotion in your notebook. This will allow you to enhance your powers of observation and description without having to juggle the demands of characterization and plot.

Following are a couple of openings that intrigued me so much I had to keep reading. The first one is from Sandra West Prowell's *When Wallflowers Die*.

> Memories slumber in dark recesses. We bury them in the coffins of our minds and think of them no more until a sound, a smell, a word resurrects them and uncovers them to the light. They live again. Embarrassment turns to laughter, grief to solace. But murder? Murder remembered tortures and haunts and bruises the soul. It lives a parallel

life to disconnected events and people that somehow pick up the stench.

(from *When Wallflowers Die,* copyright 1996 by Sandra West Prowell. Reprinted with permission from Walker & Co., 435 Hudson St., New York, NY 10014, 1-800-289-2553. All rights reserved.)

This is not a paragraph of action, but it shows what a good writer can do in a few lines of narrative to grab the reader's attention.

The second opening is from Charlaine Harris's *Dead Over Heels.*

My bodyguard was mowing the yard wearing her pink bikini when the man fell from the sky. I was occupied with adjusting the angle of the back of my folding "lounger," which I'd erected with some difficulty on the patio.

I had some warning, since I'd been aware of the buzzing of the plane for several seconds while I struggled between totally prone and rigidly upright. But Angel had one of those little tape players strapped to her waist (the plastic belt looked strange with the bikini) and the headphones and the drone of the lawn mower made her oblivious to the unusual persistence of the noise.

Circling low, I thought with some annoyance. I figured an aviator had spotted Angel and was making the most of his lucky day. Meantime, the ice in my coffee was melting and my book was lying on the little lawn table unread, while I wrestled with the stupid chair. Finally succeeding in locking the

back of the lounger into a position approximating comfort, I looked up just in time to see something large falling from the little plane, something that rotated horribly, head over heels.
(Reprinted by permission of Scribner, a Division of Simon & Schuster, from *Dead Over Heels* by Charlaine Harris. Copyright 1996 by Charlaine Harris Schultz.)

For the past few years, I've been collecting good opening lines. Following are some of the ones I've copied into my own notebook.

Some women give birth to murderers, some go to bed wit h them, and some marry them.—BEFORE THE FACT by Francis Iles

The last camel died at noon.—KEY TO REBECCA by Ken Follett.

Sheriff Dan Rhodes knew it was going to be a bad day when Bert Ramsey brought in the arm and laid it on the desk.—SHOTGUN SATURDAY NIGHT by Bill Crider.

I was trapped in a house with a lawyer, a barebreasted woman, and a dead man. The rattlesnake in the paper sack only complicated matters.—FAT TUESDAY by Earl Emerson.

His child was on the ledge.—DEAD BOLT by Jay Brandon.

"Suppose," it said, in its voice like antique silk, faded and slightly torn, *"that I could make you popular."*—THE CHEERLEADER (young adult novel) by Caroline B. Cooney.

"Once again," the man said, pulling the little girl along by the leash tied to his wrist and hers. *"Tell me your name."*—PRIMARY JUSTICE by William Bernhardt.

"Makeup can do a lot for a woman, but cannot cover a black eye."—BLIND TRUST by Linda Grant.

One of these days I'm going to take a three-day seminar on assertiveness training.—ROLL OVER AND PLAY DEAD by Joan Hess.

I began to shiver when the paramedics put the old man on a stretcher and covered up his face.—HIT AND RUN by Maxine O'Callaghan.

"Spring always brings out the suicides," the girl said, and laughed as she passed him. —DREAMLAND by M. K. Lorens.

I awoke with foreboding.—BLOOD SPORT by Dick Francis.

Some days are better than others for walking in graveyards.—NO BODY by Nancy Pickard.

A final word about openings. Check yours against the following:

- Does the first sentence contain a good narrative hook?

- Does your opening scene show an interesting character or characters in action? If not, are you sure the narrative is intriguing enough to keep the reader reading?

- Does your opening establish a viewpoint?

- Have you used fresh images, cut out tired, overused phrases and used strong verbs and nouns with a minimum of adjectives and adverbs?

CHAPTER 9

PLOT

The big question with beginning writers seems to be: To outline or not to outline. I suspect if you asked twenty published mystery writers how they do it, you'd find authors who say "I get an idea or a vague scene in mind and just start writing" and others who write detailed chapter-by-chapter outlines before they start the book itself. It really boils down to whatever works for you.

A writer who was going to teach a mystery writing course posted to one of the America-On-Line writers club boards, asking other writers how they plotted. Here are a few of the answers that were posted in reply:

From Susan Holtzer—"For what it's worth, I usually start with a scenario. For instance, in my first book, *Something to Kill For*, I wanted to write about murder on the garage-sale circuit (where I was spending a great deal of time). I started by figuring out why someone in that particular milieu would kill someone else. In my second, *Curly Smoke*, I remembered a lovely little enclave in downtown Ann Arbor that disappeared under the wrecking ball, and I wanted to 'save it.' And for my third, I thought it would be cool to kill someone in the middle of Michigan Stadium. I also had what I think is a really gonzo finale—so all I had to do (yeah, right) was fill in the middle. For me at least, once the basic scenario is established, it begins to suggest plot ideas—the kind of people who might populate that milieu, the kinds of events that might occur...and like that."

From an AOL Short Story Instructor—"I start with the ending, usually the last line. Plotting a novel usually takes me a few hours once I know the ending. Same with short stories. Ending first, and the rest is easy. Once I outline chapter by chapter, I breeze through it, three chapters a week. A look at my outline every morning tells me what I have to do for that day. Have never suffered writer's block because I do outline."

From Barbara Burnett Smith—"My ex-father-in-law was Thomas B. Dewey, creator of the Mac and Pete Schofield series, as well as several stand alones. (About 30 books total) Tom always said that if he knew the ending of the book, why would he bother to write it? He did not plot in advance, which made it more fun for him. I also write mysteries and, unfortunately, his bit of wisdom stuck.

When I start to write I have a vague idea of plot in my head, kind of like a semi-planned vacation. A few of the 'highlights' are firm. Some scenes are vivid, but only a few. How I get to each will be discovered as I write. In my second book, I had a character, sort of a young Sundance Kid, and his escape from prison, as reported by the protagonist on a small town radio station, was my focus. The complete story grew out of my fingertips each day. (Boy, is that simplistic!) Number Three is making me nuts because this time, at 62,000 words, I'm having real doubts about this murderer—he could be innocent! Is that a failure of plot or character?"

From a Writers Club regular—"Plotting has consistently been a hot topic with Rocky Mountain Fiction Writers, the group I belong to. In a recent workshop, Diane Mott Davidson said she always does a brief outline of her mystery before she starts. She said that people frequently ask why some well-known authors don't outline (like Tony Hillerman). Diane said that Wolfgang Puck may not use a written recipe, but he knows what he's doing when he cooks a dish and she thinks that experienced writers know where they're going without outlines. However, she does recommend it for beginners. Other authors said they simply can't outline, but they do know who the murderer is and why the murderer committed the crime and they back up the book from there."

From "Martha Carr."—"I always suggest to new writers to start with a well-defined character or characters and then decide what happened to them. It makes it easier to know how the plot will go. I plot out about three or four chapters ahead, in detail towards the end, and I know the ending in advance. It's the only way things can go naturally for me. My pen name is Martha Randolph Carr. The book I wrote is *Wired*, and after many failed deals and much thicker skin, *Wired* is being picked up by Hollywood."

From E. Harbison—"The wonderful mystery writer M. L. Gamble is a friend of mine and as far as plotting goes, she is always reminding me that motivation is the most important thing. So if you start with the end; i.e., the bad guy's motivation, and it's totally solid, the rest of the plot grows from there."

As you can see from these remarks, most writers at least have in mind a victim, a murderer, and a motive before they start, and maybe a few of the important things that will happen along the way.

I start with a stimulus—a quote, a spark from a newspaper article, an idea that intrigues me. I like to have the opening scene and the climactic scene (however vague) in mind before I start. But I rarely have anything in writing except for a cast of characters with a short paragraph about each. The paragraph includes a physical description, profession, age, marital status, close friends, relationship to other characters, what makes the character a suspect (if he is), etc.

Some writers strike a compromise between outlining and not outlining. That is, they outline as they go along. For example, they might estimate they'll have twenty chapters, so they write the numbers 1 through 20 with spaces between on three or four sheets of paper. Then, as they're writing, when they get little flashes and notions, they think, "That will probably come somewhere in the last half of the book," so they jot it down under Chapter 15. It may get moved to another chapter later. They may wait until each character is introduced, and then do a brief bio on him on a separate Cast of Characters sheet. They also note in each chapter, as they go along, the date, day of the week, and how much time is covered in that chapter. They may keep a rough map so that each time a scene is set, they can locate the setting on the map.

Other writers outline two or three chapters ahead because that's all they know at that point. When they finish those chapters, they can usually outline the next chapter or two. They go as far as they can see, and when they get there they can see a little farther. These chapter "outlines" can be anything from a few brief notes to several paragraphs for a chapter.

The benefit of having an outline, especially for beginning writers, is that it gives you a feeling of security.

Things may change along the way, but at least you have something to refer to. An outline may cut down on writing yourself into corners and dead ends and having to go back to some earlier place in the story and start again.

As I've said, I start with an idea or a scenario or unusual motive or method of murder. One idea that's always intrigued me is somebody masquerading as somebody else—using somebody else's name, living somebody else's life. That's the idea that sparked my first Iris House mystery, *Blooming Murder*. Once I knew that I wanted to use that idea, I began asking myself questions. Who is masquerading as somebody else? Whose identity has he/she taken over? Why? I decided that the masquerader was a young woman. Would she kill to keep from being unmasked?

I decided that, yes, she would, so I had to give her very strong motivations for doing so. Then I had to decide who the victim was. Obviously somebody who threatened to expose the masquerader's true identity. How did she find out that the young woman isn't who she says she is? What does she do about it? I decided the victim tried to blackmail the young woman to keep quiet. That meant she had to need money badly. Since the murder takes place at Iris House on the opening weekend, and both murderer and victim are guests, the murderer has to find a weapon at hand. She uses a cake knife taken from the gazebo in the back yard where the local garden club is conducting tours of the Iris gardens and serving tea.

Then I went back to the victim. Who else might want her dead and why? And who had means and opportunity to kill the victim? Stories grew around other characters who had good reason to want the victim dead. These became subplots. One suspect is the victim's cousin, and the victim knows a deep, dark secret about the suspect. She might kill to keep her cousin quiet. Another suspect thinks the victim is having an affair with her husband. And so on. For me, at this point in a book there are still lots of maybe's and question marks around all the suspects, but you need four or five suspects and clues and false clues (red herrings) that point to first one and then another of them.

For me, that's where my subplots usually come from. A subplot is a minor story line that weaves through the main story line. It should be somehow tied to the main plot and should enhance it. A subplot can be introduced whenever it best fits into the story, but almost certainly in the first half of the book. In a police procedural, one of the subplots is often a second case the detectives are working; it probably won't be a murder, unless it's going to turn out that it's tied to the main murder plot.

Subplots can be used to deepen the characterization of minor characters. One might involve a suspect and a secret that person is hiding, which may have nothing to do with the murder itself, but can cause the suspect to lie and hinder the investigation. It may be a love story that emerges during the investigation between two of the characters. If the main plot is grim, a subplot can be used to lighten the atmosphere from time to time, and serve to provide breathing space. It might even add to the suspense by leaving the reader wondering, for a short interval, what's going to happen next in the main story line.

My mysteries usually run about 75,000 words. That's roughly 300 manuscript pages. When considering the book's structure, I mentally break it down into thirds (about 100 pages per section). I want a climax, or turning point, at the end of each of the three sections. Each section builds to its own turning point.

The first section (first 100 pages) begins with the opening hook. In those first few paragraphs, you hook the reader with action, something happening and a character worth caring about. If you feel a narrative paragraph or two would be best to start with—to set the scene, for example—it should hint at something sinister to come.

Most beginning writers start too soon or start with too much background or long character descriptions. The reader is not willing to wade through much of that until he sees something happening. So don't waste time. Keep the opening simple and catchy. Later you and your readers will have time to take a breath while you fill them in on the why's and wherefore's of what they've been reading. But at the beginning, concentrate on hooking them.

Once you've grabbed the reader's attention, the first third of your book should introduce the sleuth, the victim, the murderer, and other main characters and show something of the suspects' relationships to the victim-to-be (or the already-victim, if you start with the murder).

If you don't start with the murder, it should happen in the first third of the book. This section builds to a turning point, something unexpected that sends the story off in a new direction. This could be a second murder. Perhaps the sleuth has narrowed his suspects down to a prime suspect, and then that person is murdered. Obviously this will send the investigation in a new direction, and the sleuth will have to re-examine his clues in light of the second murder.

The second section (second 100 pages) shows the sleuth exploring the "new direction" that resulted from the end of the first section of the book. This section develops suspects and interrogations, lays down clues, and introduces any subplots not introduced already. The sleuth runs into problems that keep him from successfully completing whatever he intends to do. These reversals cause tension and conflict because they alter the path he must take to get to his goal.

Meg Chittenden, author of many novels as well as *How to Write Your Novel* (published by The Writer, Inc.), says to pay close attention in this middle section, to the law of cause and effect, which should govern what happens. Instead of thinking, And then what? Meg says, think,What would happen because of this? and What would be the direct result of that?

All of this leads to the second climax or turning point. It may, for example, be a confrontation when the sleuth is physically threatened. Or maybe he confronts the person he now thinks is the killer, questions him, checks out his answers, and learns he's got the wrong person. Again, he has to go back over the clues, looking for something he may have missed before that will lead him to the real killer.

In the last third of the book, the sleuth begins to look at things in different ways. He eliminates some suspects and eventually zeroes in on the killer. The climax of this section is the big scene when the killer is revealed. Then comes the conclusion, which should be brief, explain how the detective arrived at the killer's identity (if you haven't already spelled it out), resolve subplots and quickly tie up any other loose ends.

It may help to think of your structure as a three-act play.

It's also helpful to determine what the climax of each act will be before you start, because it gives you something to aim for.

Here's what goes into each section:

Act 1

Opening hook

Introduce the sleuth.

Introduce the victim, murderer, other main characters
suspects, and possibly a subplot or two.

Show something of the suspects' relationships to the
victim.

Discovery of the body

First act climax (something unexpected that turns
things around, sends the story in a new direction)

Act 2

Develop suspects, interrogations

Lay down clues

Introduce remaining subplots

Sleuth suffers reversals in his investigation which
causes tension and conflict because they alter the
path the sleuth must take to reach his goal.

Second act climax

Act 3

Because of what happened in the second act climax,
the sleuth has to go back over the clues, trying to
find the real killer. He's looking at things in
different ways.

Sleuth eliminates suspects, zeroes in on killer.

Third act climax—killer revealed.

Conclusion —make it brief, tie up loose ends quickly.

Some writers break their plot down into four parts, or acts. Dale Furutani has said that he used the Lester Dent Master Fiction Plot as a pattern for his award-winning first mystery, *Death in Little Tokyo*. Lester Dent was a pulp fiction writer in the 1930's. Although his four-part plot outline was intended for pulp short stories, Dale adapted it for his novel.

Dent's Master Fiction Plot is included in an appendix.

CHAPTER 10

THE FIRST DRAFT

It is much easier to start a novel than to finish it. Often in the middle of a book, the author begins to listen to that nasty little critic who resides in the left side of his brain. The critic says things like, "This is really awful. Nobody will want to read this. What made you think you could be a writer in the first place? Besides, you've already got an idea for a new book that you're excited about. Why don't you abandon this one and start the new book?"

This happens to most writers I know, even those who have published many books. Don't listen to that voice! You cannot be critical and creative at the same time. You may listen to the critic when you rewrite, but not on the first draft because he will cause your imagination to shut down.

If you are really serious about being a novelist, then set a writing schedule and stick to it. I am a morning person. I rise early, have breakfast, and go immediately to my office to write. Maybe you have small children who are around all day or maybe you have an outside job. Then your best time will probably be sometime in the evening. It doesn't matter what time you choose, but you are not being unreasonable to expect to have a few uninterrupted hours a day to write. It's a matter of priority, and you may have to give up some other activity in order to have your writing time.

The key word is determination. There are thousands, maybe millions, of good writers in the world who are unpublished. The main difference between them and the writers who publish is that the latter were persistent, determined to keep writing in the face of rejections. Sometimes they wrote several books before their first sale. They *wanted* it more than all those unpublished writers.

I have found that setting a daily page quota is more effective than setting a certain amount of time to write each day. Your page quota will depend on your life. If you have an outside job, you may be able to write only two pages a day. If you're home all day and your children are in school, you can probably write five or six pages a day. Even if you write only one page a day (that's about 250 words) and take off for a vacation and the major holidays, you'll have a 300-page manuscript by the end of the year. So decide on your best writing time, set your page quota, and stick with it until you finish the first draft.

Some days it will be like digging out embedded teeth to

get words on paper. Just keep writing. I've learned from experience that *the act of writing generates inspiration.* If you hang around unpublished writers very long, you will hear someone say, "I can't write unless I'm inspired." For some time after I started selling, I heard people say that, and I'd wish I had the luxury of waiting for inspiration. But I had a contract deadline. So I'd trundle into my office every morning, a big mug of coffee in hand, and sit in front of my computer and write *something.* Finally, maybe three or four pages into the day's stint, some pretty good prose would start to appear on the screen. It wasn't ready for anybody's eyes but mine yet, but it was promising raw material. I was on the right track. Then suddenly I'd know why the scene I'd been wrestling with for the past hour wasn't working or how I was going to get my detective out of the terrible predicament he was in.

After this happened several times, I had a revelation. If I hadn't been sitting at my computer writing, I would never have found the right track and those brainstorms wouldn't have come. Waiting for inspiration to strike before you sit down to write is getting the cart before the horse. You get inspired *while* you're writing.

I don't pretend to understand it, but there is something about the *process* of writing that wakes your imagination from its lazy slumber. Your imagination is like an unused muscle. If you suddenly start to exercise it, it will give you all kinds of grief. You will not like it, and you will be tempted to quit. But if you keep exercising a lazy muscle on a regular basis, the pain will eventually go away, and the muscle will become hard and fit.

So it is with your imagination. After a while, if you stay at the computer writing, it will begin to feed you little tidbits of good stuff.

Not only is your imagination lazy, it also has a perverse sense of humor. After several days of struggling through dry-as-dust prose with nary a peep from your imagination, it will decide to stir in the middle of the night, wake you up and give you a great idea.

So don't listen to those negative voices in your head that tell you you've been meaning to clean out that file cabinet for fifteen years and now would be a good time, or you really should mop the kitchen floor or arrange all the books on your shelves in alphabetical order by author. Ignore, also, the voices that point out that writing is so much harder than you thought it would be and, besides, you can't say *that*. What will your mother think?

Blot out all those negative, demoralizing voices, and start getting something—anything—down on paper. Do this at least five days a week. The first draft won't be the best you can do, but you can fix it later. That's what revision is for. For now, just write, finish the book.

CHAPTER 11

REVISING AND REWRITING

Good books aren't just written. They're rewritten. This may be tough to accept. Surely writers who've published numerous books, who've been at it for years, can get it right the first time. Nope. Nobody gets it right the first time.

When you think about it, though, this gives you tremendous freedom. You can grant yourself permission to be really *bad* on the first draft, to just write as honestly and truly as you can without worrying about *how* you're saying it or what your mother will think.

You needn't worry about *anything* because this is only the first draft. Which turns out to be exactly the attitude you have to take to be the best writer you're capable of being. So write all the flowery, angst-ridden prose you want. After all, nobody is going to see this but you. Let it all hang out. You can clean it up later.

Finish the first draft, then put it away for a few weeks.

This will give you some distance and problems will be easier to spot.

Here are some things to think about as you go through the first draft.

1. Make sure your opening is effective, that it hooks the reader.
2. Make sure each chapter ends with a little hook of its own—something that surprises the reader or makes him want to find out what happens next.
3. Make sure you've added enough descriptive details to each scene so that the reader can visualize it.
4. Read sections aloud. Awkward prose and untrue dialogue become more apparent when read aloud (perhaps to a friend or a small critique group). Reading aloud will also make you aware of boring stretches.
5. Look for clichés which can be changed and images which can be improved. Examine each scene to see if you can (without forcing it) involve one of the five senses.
6. Check your verbs. Make them stronger, more active, if you can. But don't overdo synonyms for "said."
7. Substitute vivid nouns for weak nouns with adjectives, when possible.
8. Dump as many adverbs as you can. Often when

you find a strong, vivid verb, you won't need the adverb, or you can reword a sentence to eliminate the adverb. Instead of saying, "She said tearfully," say, "As she talked, tears filled her eyes." "Sam walked angrily from the room," could be changed to "Sam stomped from the room." If he stomps, the reader knows he's angry.

9. Get rid of as many present participles as you can (words that end in "ing." "She was running." "They were laughing." Better: "She ran." "They laughed."

10. Get rid of wastebasket words. Don't use "it," "just," or "very" too much. If you use "it" make sure it's clear what "it" refers to. For example. "He took a pencil from his pocket and broke it." Broke what, the pocket? Reword such sentences. "He reached into his pocket for a pencil and broke it." "Very" and "just" can be used occasionally in dialogue, but try to keep them out of the rest of your manuscript.

11. Look for repetitive words. If a word appears twice in a sentence or even in a short paragraph, find a synonym.

12. Check for sentence length. You need some variety—not all short sentences, not all long sentences, but a mix of both.

13. Concentrate on "showing" rather than "telling."

"She was frightened" is telling. "Her heart hammered in her ears and her hands shook as she moved the curtain slightly to peer into the dark" is showing. All important scenes should be shown (moment by moment) rather than told. For a detailed discussion of how to write scenes, I recommend Dwight Swain's book *Techniques of the Selling Writer*, published by the University of Oklahoma Press.

14. Make sure you haven't inadvertently stepped out of viewpoint. Use only one viewpoint per chapter or scene. If two scenes in two different viewpoints appear in the same chapter, add some white space between them.

15. Make sure you have your facts straight and that, for example, the eye color of a character doesn't change half-way through the book.

16. Make sure your chapters don't all start the same way— with dialogue, description or any particular device.

17. Make sure your characters' motivations are strong, clear and credible.

18. Check your pacing. One reason manuscripts get turned down today is that they move too slowly. To speed up pace, use more short sentences and short paragraphs; skip transitional material between scenes (finish one scene, add some white space, and

go directly to the next scene); and tighten the manuscript throughout by cutting out superfluous words.

CHAPTER 12

MARKETING YOUR BOOK

PROPER MANUSCRIPT FORM

Use the proper format for your novel manuscript. It should be typed, double-spaced, on good white, letter-size bond paper with one-inch margins on both sides and at the bottom. At the top of the first page of your manuscript, near the top edge, type your name and address (single-spaced) on the left, and on the right near the top edge should be the approximate number of words in the manuscript. (For example: About 75,000 words) On the first page, you should leave plenty of white space after these headings. One-third to one-half of the way down the page, type your title centered in all caps. Below that type "by" and your name or pen name. Below the by-line, type your chapter heading.

On the second and subsequent pages, your header at the top, just below the edge of the page, should have your name on the left and, on the right, the title of the book and the page number. Leave four or five spaces between the header and the text. On the last page of your manuscript type "THE END" below the last line of text. (See appendices for sample manuscript pages.)

SYNOPSIS

Now that your manuscript is ready to go, it's time to think about marketing it. You will need a synopsis of no more than ten double-spaced pages. It should be written in the present tense. (Example: When two children disappear from the small town of Marle, TX, the town is in a panic.) You might pattern it after the book reports you wrote in school. The synopsis should tell the important events that occur in the story. You won't have room for much dialogue, description, etc.

Many beginning mystery writers ask if they have to tell the ending in the synopsis. The answer is yes. I've heard too many editors say it irritates them to be reading a synopsis and, when they get to the end, discover that the writer has withheld the identity of the murderer. The editor may not have the full manuscript, and she wants to know that *you* know how the book will end.

QUERY LETTER

Address your query letter to a specific editor or agent. Do your homework. If necessary, call the editorial or agency office and ask, "To whom do I send a query for a mystery novel?" Or check the current *Writer's Market* or *Literary Market Place.* Be sure the spelling of his/her name and title is correct.

Use conservative letterhead (or, if you don't have that, use plain white paper with some rag content). Do not use a dot matrix printer. The letter should be typed or printed on a laser printer or other typewriter-quality printer. It should be free of typos, misspellings and grammar errors. Be neat and professional.

Single space the letter. This is not a manuscript.

Under no circumstances should a query letter be longer than two pages. One page is preferable. Don't try to dazzle. Be direct and honest.

Tell what your book is about in a paragraph or two. This description should resemble the book cover copy used on published paperback books.

Mention previous encounters with the editor or agent, if any. Or say where you got the individual's name (from the *Literary Market Place*, for example). If you got the name from a client, don't mention that name without the client's permission. If your book is similar to a book you know the agent has represented or the editor has edited, mention that.

In one paragraph, near the end of the letter, mention your credits, if any, or say why you are uniquely qualified to write this book. (For example, you've been a high school teacher for ten years and your sleuth is a high school teacher).

Say that you have a finished manuscript. If the agent or editor is interested, he/she will probably first ask to see a synopsis and the first two chapters.

End with something like, "I'll be glad to send you a synopsis and sample chapters or the entire manuscript. Please let me know if you're interested."

Enclose a self-addressed, stamped envelope for the reply. (A sample query letter is included in an appendix.)

WHERE TO SEND THE QUERY LETTER

It can be difficult to sell a book without an agent. Many publishing houses won't even look at unagented manuscripts. I always advise students to query agents first. If you know any published writers, they may be willing to give you the names and addresses of their agents to query. Also, you'll find agents listed in *Writer's Market* and *Literary Market Place*. Both of these can probably be found in your library. Read the entries under "Literary Agencies" to find out what kind of books each agency represents and what they've sold recently. Make a list of all agents and agencies who say they represent mysteries.

Then begin sending out your query letter. You can multiple submit the query letter (not the manuscript).

If you have met an editor (at a conference, for example) you can try querying the editor directly. Be sure to mention where you met him/her. Another way to get a manuscript read by an editor is to enter one of the two mystery novel contests for unpublished writers sponsored each year by St. Martin's Press. One is for a private eye novel, the other is for a traditional mystery, which basically includes any kind of whodunit except for the P. I. novel.

For contest guidelines, write St. Martin's Press, 175 Fifth Avenue, New York, NY 10010.

CHAPTER 13

NOW WHAT?

Once your manuscript is ready for submitting and you've begun sending out queries, don't sit back and wait. Don't tie up all your emotions, your hopes and dreams, in one manuscript.

You probably already have an idea for a new book. Give yourself a few days or weeks off, then start the next book.

There are few guarantees in the writing business, but one thing is certain. The more you write, the better writer you'll be. You won't notice the difference, day to day; but if you're writing regularly, when you look at something you wrote six or eight months previously, you'll see the improvement.

So write regularly and trust the process.

Finally, good luck!

Appendix A
PROPER MANUSCRIPT FORM

Jean Hager
Street Address   About 75,000 words
City, State, Zip

BLOOMING MURDER

by

Jean Hager

Chapter 1

A click as soft as a whisper broke the silence of the

April night. Tess Darcy awoke abruptly, aware that a sound

had roused her from the deep sleep of exhaustion.

She stared at the moonlight-washed wall opposite her

brass bed, trying to get her bearings. Perhaps Primrose was

having a restless night. She slid out of bed quietly, padded

to the door, and switched on the hall light. No sign of the

cat.

She moved down the hall and peered into the dim

sitting room. The gray Persian was curled in her favorite

chair, which featured a Renaissance Revival design with a

medallion on top and a comfortably padded seat. Tess had

given up trying to keep her out of it. At the moment,
Primrose was dead to the world. Tess hesitated. What had
awakened her?

Puzzled, she glanced at her watch, which read one-ten,
and retraced her steps, turning off the hall light as she
passed the switch.

She had grown accustomed to being in the house alone
at night, so possibly she'd heard one of her guests moving
about upstairs. All seven of them had checked in last
evening for tomorrow's official opening day of Iris House,
Tess's brand-new bed and breakfast.

She crawled back into bed, hoping she could fall asleep
again quickly. She needed to be rested for what was certain
to be a hectic day.

As she sighed and drew the bed sheet over her, she
caught the movement of a shadow on the moonlit wall of her
bedroom. Alarmed, Tess shot to a sitting position. Was
that a tree branch? But there was no wind, and besides, it
didn't look like a branch.

As Tess stared, the ghostly figure of a woman in a
long, flowing garment floated across the wall in the
drenching moonlight. Whoever was casting the shadow was
outside, behind the house.

Appendix B
SAMPLE QUERY LETTER

Jane Doe
Street Address
City/State/Zip
Phone/Fax

(Date)

Betty Boop
Boop Literary Agency
7 East Avenue
New York, NY 10010

Dear Ms. Boop:

My novel, *Dead Before Morning*, is the first in a planned series featuring Kate Dooley, a private investigator. In *Dead Before Morning*, Kate agrees to tackle her first murder investigation when Unique Technology's star software engineer is found dead. Armed with a tendency to be overly polite and a Smith and Wesson semi-automatic, Kate quickly discovers that much about the high-tech establishment is peculiar: the company is housed in a restored warehouse widely rumored to be haunted, its president appears to be psychotic, and the employees tend to be jealous and vengeful. Even the dead man refuses to remain dead, or at least troubling memos from him, dated after his death, continue to appear, eventually assisting Kate in tracking down the murderer. To complicate matters, Kate's best friend, Laurie, cheerfully persists in offering unwanted advice as Kate copes with both a recent divorce and her attraction to a former colleague of the deceased.

I worked for eleven years as a software engineer and am currently working full-time on a second Kate Dooley mystery.

I am seeking representation for *Dead Before Morning* and would be happy to send you the manuscript (75,000 words) or sample chapters and a synopsis. I enclose a SASE for your reply.

Thank you for your time and consideration.

Sincerely,

105

APPENDIX C

Lester Dent Master Fiction Plot
(Originally published in the 1936 Writer's Digest Yearbook)

This is a formula, a master plot, for any 6000 word pulp story. It has worked on adventure, detective, western and war-air. It tells exactly where to put everything. It shows definitely just what must happen in each successive thousand words.

No yarn of mine written to the formula has yet failed to sell.

The business of building stories seems not much different from the business of building anything else.

Here's how it starts:
1. A DIFFERENT MURDER METHOD FOR VILLAIN TO USE
2. A DIFFERENT THING FOR VILLAIN TO BE SEEKING
4. A DIFFERENT LOCALE
4. A MENACE WHICH HANGS LIKE A CLOUD OVER HERO

One of these DIFFERENT things would be nice, two better, three swell. It may help if they are fully in mind before tackling the rest.

A different murder method could be—different. Thinking of shooting, knifing, garroting, poison needles, scorpions, a few others, and writing them on paper gets them where they may suggest something. Scorpions and their poison bite? Maybe mosquitos or flies treated with deadly germs?

If the victims are killed by ordinary methods, but found under strange and identical circumstances each time, it might serve, the reader of course not knowing until the end, that the method of murder is ordinary. Scribes who have their villain's victims found with butterflies, spiders or bats stamped on them could conceivably be flirting with this gag.

Probably it won't do a lot of good to be too odd, fanciful or grotesque with murder methods.

The different thing for the villain to be after might be something other than jewels, the stolen bank loot, the pearls, or some other old

106

ones. Here, again, one might get too bizarre.

Unique locale? Easy. Selecting one that fits in with the murder method and the treasure—thing that villain wants—makes it simpler, and it's also nice to use a familiar one, a place where you've lived or worked. It sometimes saves embarrassment to know nearly as much about the locale as the editor, or enough to fool him.

Divide the 6000 word yarn into four 1500 word parts. In each 1500 word part, put the following:

FIRST 1500 WORDS

1—First line, or as near thereto as possible, introduce the hero and swat him with a fistful of trouble. Hint at a mystery, a menace or a problem to be solved—something the hero has to cope with.

2—The hero pitches in to cope with his fistful of trouble. (He tries to fathom the mystery, defeat the menace, or solve the problem.)

3—Introduce ALL the other characters as soon as possible. Bring them on in action.

4. Hero's endeavors land him in an actual physical conflict near the end of the first 1500 words.

5—Near the end of first 1500 words, there is a complete surprise twist in the plot development.

SO FAR: Does it have SUSPENSE?
              Is there a MENACE to the hero?
              Does everything happen logically?

At this point, it might help to recall that action should do something besides advance the hero over the scenery. Suppose the hero has learned the dastards of villains have seized somebody named Eloise, who can explain the secret of what is behind all these sinister events. The hero corners villains, they fight, and villains get away. Not so hot.

Hero should accomplish something with his tearing around, if only

107

to rescue Eloise, and surprise! Eloise is a ring-tailed monkey. The hero counts the rings on Eloise's tail, if nothing better comes to mind. They're not real. The rings are painted there. Why?

SECOND 1500 WORDS

1—Shovel more grief onto the hero.

2—Hero, being heroic, struggles, and his struggles lead up to:

3—Another physical conflict.

4—A surprising plot twist to end the 1500 words.

NOW: Does second part have SUSPENSE?
Does the MENACE grow like a black cloud?
Is the hero getting it in the neck?
Is the second part logical?

DON'T TELL ABOUT IT—Show how the thing looked. This is one of the secrets of writing; never tell the reader—show him. (He trembles, roving eyes, slackened jaw, and such.) MAKE THE READER SEE HIM.

When writing, it helps to get at least one minor surprise to the printed page. It is reasonable to expect these minor surprises to sort of inveigle the reader into keeping on. They need not be such profound efforts. One method of accomplishing one now and then is to be gently misleading. Hero is examining the murder room. The door behind him begins slowly to open. He does not see it. He conducts his examination blissfully. Door eases open, wider and wider, until—surprise! The glass pane falls out of the big window across the room. It must have fallen slowly, and air blowing into the room caused the door to open. Then what the heck made the pane fall so slowly? More mystery.

Characterizing a story actor consists of giving him some things which make him stick in the reader's mind. TAG HIM.

BUILD PLOTS SO THAT ACTION CAN BE CONTINUOUS.

108

THIRD 1500 WORDS

1—Shovel the grief onto the hero.

2—Hero makes some headway, and corners the villain or somebody in:

3—A physical conflict.

4—A surprising plot twist, in which the hero preferably gets it in the neck bad, to end the 1500 words.

DOES: It still have SUSPENSE?
        The MENACE get blacker?
        The hero find himself in a hell of a fix?
        It all happen logically?

These outlines or master formulas are only something to make you certain of inserting some physical conflict, and some genuine plot twists, with a little suspense and menace thrown in. Without them, there is no pulp story.

These physical conflicts in each part might be DIFFERENT, too. If one fight is with fists, that can take care of the pugilism until the next yarn. Same for poison gas and swords. There may, naturally, be exceptions. A hero with a peculiar punch, or a quick draw, might use it more than once.

The idea is to avoid monotony.

ACTION:
Vivid, swift, no words wasted. Create suspense, make the reader see and feel the action.

ATMOSPHERE:
Hear, smell, see, feel and taste.

DESCRIPTION:
Trees, wind, scenery and water.

THE SECRET, MAKE EVERY WORD COUNT.

FOURTH 1500 WORDS

1—Shovel the difficulties more thickly upon the hero.

2—Get the hero almost buried in his troubles. (Figuratively, the villain has him prisoner and has him framed for a murder rap; the girl is presumably dead, everything is lost, and the DIFFERENT murder method is about to dispose of the suffering protagonist.)

3—The hero extricates himself using HIS OWN SKILL, training or brawn.

4—The mysteries remaining—one big one held over to this point will help grip interest—are cleared up in course of final conflict as hero takes the situation in hand.

5—Final twist, a big surprise. (This can be the villain turning out to be the unexpected person, having the "Treasure" be a dud, etc.)

6—The snapper, the punch line to end it.

HAS: The SUSPENSE held out to the last line?
      The MENACE held out to the last?
      Everything been explained?
      It all happened logically?
      The last line enough punch to leave the reader with
            that WARM FEELING?
      The hero captured or killed the villain? (Not God or
            coincidence)?

Appendix D
MYSTERY AWARD WINNERS

AGATHA AWARDS
(Chosen annually by a vote of registrants at the Malice Domestic conference to honor "mysteries of manners" in two categories.)

Best Mystery Novel
1997-*Up Jumps the Devil* by Margaret Maron
1996-*If I'd Killed Him When I Met Him*
     by Sharyn McCrumb
1995-*She Walks These Hills* by Sharyn McCrumb
1994-*Dead Man's Island* by Carolyn Hart
1993-*Bootlegger's Daughter* by Margaret Maron
1992-*I.O.U.* by Nancy Pickard
1991-*Bum Steer* by Nancy Pickard
1990-*Naked Once More* by Elizabeth Peters
1989-*Something Wicked* by Carolyn Hart

Best First Mystery
1997-*Murder on a Girl's Night Out* by Anne George
1996-*The Body in the Transept* by Jeanne M. Dams
1995-*Do Unto Others* by Jeff Abbott
1994-*Track of the Cat* by Nevada Barr
1993-*Blanche on the Lam* by Barbara Neely
1992-*Zero at the Bone* by Mary Willis Walker
1991-*The Body in the Belfry* by Katherine Hall Page
1990-*Grime and Punishment* by Jill Churchill
1989-*A Great Deliverance* by Elizabeth George

ANTHONY AWARDS

(Chosen by vote of registrants at the annual Bouchercon World Mystery Convention. Award named for the late Anthony Boucher, well-known writer, critic, and fan of the mystery genre.)

Best Mystery Novel

1997-*The Poet* by Michael Connelly
1996-*Under the Beetle's Cellar* by Mary Willis Walker
1995-*She Walks These Hills* by Sharyn McCrumb
1994-*Wolf in the Shadows* by Marcia Muller
1993-*Bootlegger's Daughter* by Margaret Maron
1992-*The Last Detective* by Peter Lovesey
1991-*"G" is For Gumshoe* by Sue Grafton
1990-*The Sirens Sang of Murder* by Sarah Caudwell
1989-*The Silence of the Lambs* by Thomas Harris
1988-*Skinwalkers* by Tony Hillerman
1987-*"C" is For Corpse* by Sue Grafton
1986-*"B" is For Burglar* by Sue Grafton

Best First Mystery

1997-Tie: *Death in Little Tokyo* by Dale Furutani
        Somebody Else's Child by Terris Grimes
1996-*Death in Bloodhound Red* by Virginia Lanier
1995-*The Alienist* by Caleb Carr
1994-*Track of the Cat* by Nevada Barr
1993-*Blanche on the Lam* by Barbara Neely
1992-*Murder on the Iditarod Trail* by Sue Henry
1991-*Postmortem* by Patricia D. Cornwell
1990-*Katwalk* by Karen Kijewski
1989-*A Great Deliverance* by Elizabeth George
1988-*Caught Dead in Philadelphia* by Gillian Roberts
1987-*Too Late To Die* by Bill Crider
1986-*When the Bough Breaks* by Jonathan Kellerman

ANTHONY AWARDS (continued)

Best Paperback Original
1997-*Fade Away* by Harlan Coben
1996-*Deal Breaker* by Harlan Coben
1991-Tie: *Grave Undertaking* by James McCahery and
        Where's Mommy Now by Rochelle Krich
1990-*Honeymoon with Murder* by Carolyn Hart
1989-*Something Wicked* by Carolyn Hart
1988-*The Monkey's Raincoat* by Robert Crais
1987-*Junkyard Dog* by Robert Campbell
1986-*Say No to Murder* by Nancy Pickard

EDGAR ALLAN POE AWARDS
(Presented annually by Mystery Writers of America.)

Best Mystery Novel
1997-*The Chatham School Affair* by Thomas H. Cook
1996-*Come to Grief* by Dick Francis
1995-*The Red Scream* by Mary Willis Walker
1994-*The Sculptress* by Minette Walters
1993-*Bootlegger's Daughter* by Margaret Maron
1992-*A Dance at the Slaughterhouse* by Lawrence Block
1991-*New Orleans Mourning* by Julie Smith
1990-*Black Cherry Blues* by James Lee Burke
1989-*A Cold Red Sunrise* by Stuart M. Kaminsky
1988-*Old Bones* by Aaron Elkins
1987-*A Dark-Adapted Eye* by Barbara Vine
1986-*The Suspect* by L. R. Wright
1985-*Briarpatch* by Ross Thomas
1984-*La Brava* by Elmore Leonard
1983-*Billingsgate Shoal* by Rick Boyer
1982-*Peregrine* by William Bayer
1981-*Whip Hand* by Dick Francis
1980-*The Rheingold Route* by Arthur Maling
1979-*The Eye of the Needle* by Ken Follett
1978-*Catch Me: Kill Me* by William H. Hallahan
1977-*Promised Land* by Robert B. Parker
1976-*Hopscotch* by Brian Garfield
1975-*Peter's Pence* by Jon Cleary
1974-*Dance Hall of the Dead* by Tony Hillerman
1972-*The Lingala Code* by Warren Kiefer
1971-*The Laughing Policeman* by Maj Sjowall
        and Per Wahloo
1970-*Forfeit* by Dick Francis
1969-*A Case of Need* by Jeffrey Hudson

EDGAR ALLAN POE AWARDS (continued)

1968-*God Save the Mark* by Donald E. Westlake
1967-*The King of the Rainy Country* by Nicholas Freeling
1966-*The Quiller Memorandum* by Adam Hall
1965-*The Spy Who Came in From the Cold*
    by John le Carré
1964-*The Light of Day* by Eric Ambler
1962-*Death and the Joyful Woman* by Ellis Peters
1961-*The Progress of a Crime* by Julian Symons
1960-*The Hours Before Dawn* by Celia Fremlin
1959-*The Eighth Circle* by Stanley Ellis
1958-*Room to Swing* by Ed Lacy
1957-*A Dram of Poison* by Charlotte Armstrong
1956-*Beast in View* by Margaret Millar
1955-*The Long Goodbye* by Raymond Chandler
1954-*Beat Not the Bones* by Charlotte Jay

Best First Mystery by an American Author
1997-*Simple Justice* by John Morgan Wilson
1996-*Penance* by David Housewright
1995-*The Caveman's Valentine* by George Dawes Green
1994-*A Grave Talent* by Laurie King
1993-*The Black Echo* by Michael Connelly
1992-*Slow Motion Riot* by Peter Blauner
1991-*Postmortem* by Patricia D. Cornwell
1990-*The Last Billable Hour* by Susan Wolfe
1989-*Carolina Skeletons* by David Stout
1988-*Death Among Strangers* by Deidre S. Laiken
1987-*No One Rides for Free* by Larry Reinhart
1986-*When the Bough Breaks* by Jonathan Kellerman
1985-*Strike Three, You're Dead* by R. D. Rosen
1984-*The Bay Psalm Book Murder* by Will Harriss

EDGAR ALLAN POE AWARDS (continued)

1983-*The Butcher's Boy* by Thomas Perry
1982-*Chiefs* by Stuart Woods
1981-*The Watcher* by K. Nolte Smith
1980-*The Lasko Tangent* by Richard North Patterson
1979-*Killed in the Ratings* by William L. DeAndrea
1978-*A French Finish* by Robert Ross
1977-*The Thomas Berryman Number* by James Patterson
1976-*The Alvarez Journal* by Rex Burns
1975-*Fletch* by Gregory Mcdonald
1974-*The Billion Dollar Sure Thing* by Paul E. Erdman
1973-*Squaw Point* by R. H. Shimer
1972-*Finding Maubee* by A. H. Z. Carr
1971-*The Anderson Tapes* by Lawrence Sanders
1970-*A Time for Predators* by Joe Gores
1969-Tie: *Silver Street* by E. Richard Johnson and
        The Bait by Dorothy Uhnak
1968-*Act of Fear* by Michael Collins
1967-*The Cold War Swap* by Ross Thomas
1966-*In the Heat of the Night* by John Ball
1965-*Friday the Rabbi Slept Late* by Harry Kemelman
1964-*Florentine Finish* by Cornelius Hirschberg
1963-*The Fugitive* by Robert L. Fish
1962-*The Green Stone* by Suzanne Blanc
1961-*The Man in the Cage* by John Holbrooke Vance
1960-*The Grey Flannel Shroud* by Henry Slesar
1959-*The Bright Road to Fear* by Richard Martin Stern
1958-*Knock and Wait a While* by William Rawle Weeks
1957-*Rebecca's Pride* by Donald McNutt Douglass
1956-*The Perfectionist* by Lane Kauffman
1955-*Go, Lovely Rose* by Jean Potts
1954-*A Kiss Before Dying* by Ira Levin

EDGAR ALLAN POE AWARDS (continued)

1953-*Don't Cry for Me* by William Campbell Gault and
    E. P. Dutton, publisher
1952-*Strangle Hold* by Mary McMullen and
    Harper Bros., publisher
1951-*Nightmare in Manhattan* by Thomas Walsh
1950-*What a Body* by Alan Green
1949-*The Room Upstairs* by Mildred David and
    Simon & Schuster, publisher
1948-*The Fabulous Clipjoint* by Fredric Brown and
    E. P. Dutton & Co, publisher
1947-*The Horizontal Man* by Helen Eustis
1946-*Watchful at Night* by Julius Fast

Best Paperback Original
1997-*Fade Away* by Harlan Coben
1996-*Tarnished Blue* by William Heffernan
1995-*Final Appeal* by Lisa Scottoline
1994-*Dead Folk's Blues* by Steven Womack
1993-*A Cold Day for Murder* by Dana Stabenow
1992-*Dark Maze* by Thomas Adcock
1991-*The Man Who Would be F. Scott Fitzgerald*
    by David Handler
1990-*The Rain* by Keith Peterson
1989-*The Telling of Lies* by Timothy Findley
1988-*Bimbos of the Death Sun* by Sharyn McCrumb
1987-*The Junkyard Dog* by Robert Campbell
1986-*Pigs Get Fat* by Warren Murphy
1985-*Grandmaster* by Warren Murphy and
    Molly Cochran
1984-*Mrs. White* by Margaret Tracy
1983-*Triangle* by Teri White

EDGAR ALLAN POE AWARDS (continued)

1982-*The Old Dick* by L. A. Morse
1981-*Public Murders* by Bill Granger
1980-*The Hog Murders* by Willliam L. DeAndrea
1979-*Deceit and Deadly Lies* by Frank Bandy
1978-*The Quark Maneuver* by Mike Jahn
1977-*Confess, Fletch* by Gregory Mcdonald
1976-*Autopsy* by John R. Feegel
1975-*The Corpse That Walked* by Roy Winsor
1974-*Death of an Informer* by Will Perry
1973-*The Invader* by Richard Wormser
1972-*For Murder I Charge More* by Frank McAuliffe
1971-*Flashpoint* by Dan J. Marlowe
1970-*The Dragon's Eye* by Scott C. S. Stone

MACAVITY AWARDS

(Chosen annually by a vote of members of Mystery Readers International. Named for the "mystery cat" of T. S. Eliot in *Old Possum's Book of Practical Cats*.)

Best Mystery Novel
1997-*Bloodhounds* by Peter Lovesey
1996-*Under the Beetle's Cellar* by Mary Willis Walker
1995-*She Walks These Hills* by Sharyn McCrumb
1994-*The Sculptress* by Minette Walters
1993-*Bootlegger's Daughter* by Margaret Maron
1992-*I. O. U.* by Nancy Pickard
1991-*If Ever I Return Pretty Peggy-O*
    by Sharyn McCrumb
1990-*A Little Class on Murder* by Carolyn Hart
1989-*A Thief of Time* by Tony Hillerman
1988-*Marriage is Murder* by Nancy Pickard
1987-*A Taste for Death* by P. D. James

Best First Mystery
1997-*Death in Little Tokyo* by Dale Furutani
1996-*The Strange Files of Fremont Jones* by Dianne Day
1995-*Do Unto Others* by Jeff Abbott
1994-*Death Comes as Epiphany* by Sharan Newman
1993-*Blanche on the Lam* by Barbara Neely
1992-Tie: *Murder on the Iditarod Trail* by Sue Henry and
    Zero at the Bone by Mary Willis Walker
1991-*Postmortem* by Patricia Cornwell
1990-*Grime and Punishment* by Jill Churchill
1989-*The Killings at Badger's Drift* by Caroline Graham
1988-*The Monkey's Raincoat* by Robert Crais
1987-Tie: *A Ritual Bath* by Faye Kellerman and
    A Case of Loyalties by Marilyn Wallace

SELECTED BIBLIOGRAPHY

BOOKS ON WRITING

The ABC's of Writing Fiction, by Ann Copeland. Story
    Press, 1996

The Art and Craft of Novel Writing, by Oakley Hall. Story
    Press, 1994

The Art of Fiction: Notes on Craft for Young Writers, by
    John Gardner. Vintage Books, 1991

The Art of Writing for Publication, by Kenneth T. Henson.
    Allyn & Bacon, 1995

Aspects of the Novel, by Edward Morgan Forster.
    Harcourt Brace, 1985

Becoming a Writer, by Dorothea Thompson Brande.
    J. P. Tarcher, 1981

Beginnings, Middles, and Ends (Elements of Fiction
    Writing), by Nancy Kress. Writer's Digest Books,
    1993

Bird by Bird: Some Instructions for Writing and Life, by
    Anne Lamott. Anchor Books, 1995

Building Fiction: How to Develop Plot and Structure,
    by J. L. Kercheval. Writer's Digest Books, 1997

Characters and Viewpoint (Elements of Fiction Writing),
    by Orson S. Card. Writer's Digest Books, 1988

Colloquium on Crime, R. Winks, ed., Scribner, 1986

Conflict, Action and Suspense (Elements of Fiction
    Writing), by William Noble. Writer's Digest
    Books, 1988

The Complete Guide to Writing Fiction, by Barnaby
    Conrad. Writer's Digest Books, 1990

The Courage to Write: How Writers Transcend Fear, by
    Ralph Keyes. Henry Holt, 1996

Creating Characters: How to Build Story People, by
    Dwight V. Swain. Writer's Digest Books, 1994

BIBLIOGRAPHY (continued)

Creating Unforgettable Characters, by Linda Seger. Henry Holt, 1990

Creative Writer's Handbook, by Philip K. Jason and Allan B. Lefcowitz. Prentice Hall, 1993

Dare to be a Great Writer: 329 Keys to Powerful Fiction, by Leonard Bishop. Writer's Digest Books, 1992

Description (Elements of Fiction Writing), by Monica Wood. Writer's Digest Books, 1995

Dialogue in Fiction (Elements of Fiction Writing), by Lewis Turco. Writer's Digest Books, 1989

The Elements of Storytelling for Writers, by Peter Rubie. John Wiley & Sons, 1996

Fiction Writer's Handbook, by Hallie Burnett and Whit Burnett. Harperperrenial Library, 1993

Get That Novel Started! (And Keep Going Til You Finish), by Donna Levin. Writer's Digest Books, 1992

How to Write Best Selling Fiction: Discover the Keys to Success in Today's Market for Novels, by Dean Koontz. Writer's Digest Boooks, 1981

How to Write Crime, Marele Day, editor. Allen & Unwin, 1996

How to Write a Damn Good Novel, Vol. I, by James N. Frey. St. Martin's Press, 1987

How to Write a Damn Good Novel, Vol. II: Advanced Techniques for Dramatic Storytelling, by James N. Frey. St. Martin's Press, 1994

How to Write & Sell Your First Novel, by Oscar Collier and Frances Spatz Leighton. Writer's Digest Books, 1997

How to Write Mysteries, by Shannon O'Cork. Writer's Digest Books, 1989

How to Write a Mystery, by Larry Beinhart. Ballantine Books, 1996

How to Write Your Novel, by Meg Chittenden. The Writer, Inc., 1995

Learning to Write Fiction from the Masters, by Barnaby Conrad. Plume, 1996

Mastering Fiction Writing, by Kit Reed. Writer's Digest Books, 1991

20 Master Plots (And How to Build Them), by Ronald B. Tobias. Writer's Digest Books, 1993

The 29 Most Common Writing Mistakes and How to Avoid Them, by Judy Detton. Writer's Digest Books, 1991

The 38 Most Common Fiction Writing Mistakes: (And How to Avoid Them), by Jack M. Bickham. Writer's Digest Books, 1997

Murder Mystique, Lucy Freeman, editor. Frederick Unger Publishing Co., 1982

On Becoming a Novelist, by John Gardner. HarperCollins 1986

Plot (Elements of Fiction Writing), by Ansen Dibell. Writer's Digest Books, 1988

Plotting and Writing Suspense Fiction, by Patricia Highsmith. St. Martin's Press, 1990

Scene and Structure (Elements of Fiction Writing), by Jack M. Bickham. Writer's Digest Books, 1993

Self-Editing for Fiction Writers, by Renni Browne and Dave King. HarperCollins, 1994

Setting/How to Create and Sustain a Sense of Time and Place in Your Fiction (Elements of Fiction Writing), by Jack Bickham. Writer's Digest, 1994

So You Want to Write a Novel, by Lou Willett Stanek. Avon Books, 1994

Spider, Spin Me a Web: A Handbook for Fiction Writers, by Lawrence Block. Wm. Morrow & Co., 1996

BIBLIOGRAPHY (continued)

Structuring Your Novel: From Basic Idea to Finished Manuscript, by Robert C. Meredith and John D. Fitzgerald. Harperperennial Library, 1993

Technique in Fiction, by Robie MacAuley and George Lanning. St. Martin's Press, 1990

Techniques of the Selling Writer, by Dwight V. Swain. University of Oklahoma Press, 1982

Telling Lies for Fun and Profit: A Manual for Fiction Writers, by Lawrence Block. Wm. Morrow & Co., 1994

Wild Mind: Living the Writer's Life, by Natalie Goldberg. Bantam Doubleday Dell, 1990

The Writer's Digest Sourcebook for Building Believable Characters, by Marc McCutcheon. Writer's Digest Books, 1996

Writing and Selling Your Novel, by Jack M. Bickham. Writer's Digest Books, 1996

Writing the Blockbuster Novel, by Albert Zuckerman. Writer's Digest Books, 1994

Writing Crime & Suspense Fiction: And Getting Published, by Lesley Grant-Adamson. Teach Yourself, 1996

Writing Crime Fiction, by H. R. F. Keating. St. Martin's Press, 1991

Writing Down the Bones, by Natalie Goldbereg. Shambhala Publications, 1986

Writing the Modern Mystery, by Barbara Norville. Writer's Digest Books, 1992

Writing Mysteries: A Handbook by the Mystery Writers of America. Writer's Digest Books, 1992

Writing the Novel: From Plot to Print, by Lawrence Block. Writer's Digest Books, 1985

BIBLIOGRAPHY (continued)

Writing the Private Eye Novel: A Handbook by the Private Eye Writers of America, Robert J. Randisi, editor. Writer's Digest Books, 1997

BOOKS FOR BACKGROUND

Amateur Detectives: A Writer's Guide to How Private Citizens Solve Criminal Cases, by Elaine Raco Chase and Anne Wingate. Writer's Digest Books, 1996

Armed and Dangerous: A Writer's Guide to Weapons, by Michael Newton. Writer's Digest Books, 1990

Body Trauma: A Writer's Guide to Wounds and Injuries, by David W. Page. Writer's Digest Books, 1996

Cause of Death: A Writer's Guide to Death, Murder and Forensic Medicine, by Keith D. Wilson. Writer's Digest Books, 1992

Criminal Evidence, by John C. Klotter. Anderson Publishing Co., 1987

Criminal Procedure for the Criminal Justice Professional, by John N. Ferdico. West Publishing Co., 1985

Dead Men Do Tell Tales, by William R. Maples, PhD., Doubleday, 1994

Deadly Doses: A Writer's Guide to Poisons, by Serita Deborah Stevens and Anne Klarner. Writer's Digest Books, 1990

Death Investigator's Handbook, by Louis N. Eliopulos. Paladin Press, 1993

Malicious Intent: A Writer's Guide to How Murderers, Robbers, Rapists and Other Criminals Think, by Sean P. MacTire. Writer's Digest Books, 1995

Missing Persons: A Writer's Guide to Finding the Lost, the Abducted and the Escaped, by Fay Faron. Writer's Digest Books, 1997

BIBLIOGRAPHY (continued)

Modus Operandi: A Writer's Guide to How Criminals Work, by Mauro V. Corvasce and Joseph R. Paglino. Writer's Digest Books, 1995

Murder One: A Writer's Guide to Homicide, by Mauro Corvasce and Joseph Paglino. Writer's Digest Books, 1997

Police Procedural: A Writer's Guide to the Police and How They Work, by Russell Bintliff. Writer's Digest Books, 1993

Private Eyes: A Writer's Guide to Private Investigating, by Hal Blythe. Writer's Digest Books, 1993

Scene of the Crime: A Writer's Guide to Crime Scene Investigations, by Anne Wingate. Writer's Digest Books, 1992

The Writer's Complete Crime Reference Book, by Martin Roth. Writer's Digest Books, 1990

OTHER BOOKS OF INTEREST

The American Dictionary of Writer's Guidelines: What Editors Want, What Editors Buy, John C. Mutchter, editor. Quill Driver Books, 1997

The Art of Editing, 6th Edition, by Floyd K. Baskette, Jack Z. Sissors, and Brian S. Brooks. Allyn & Bacon, 1996

Be Your Own Literary Agent: The Ultimate Insider's Guide to Getting Published, by Martin P. Levin. Ten Speed Press, 1995

The Complete Guide to Self-Publishing, by Tom and Marilyn Ross. Writer's Digest Books, 1994

Guide to Literary Agents (Annual), Donald M. Pruess, editor. Writer's Digest Books

BIBLIOGRAPHY (continued)

How to Be Your Own Literary Agent: The Business of Getting a Book Published, by Richard Curtis. Houghton Mifflin Co., 1996

Literary Agents: What They Do, How They Do It, and How To Find and Work with the Right One for You, by Michael Larsen. John Wiley & Sons, 1996

Mystery Writer's Sourcebook: Where to Sell Your Manuscripts, David H. Borcherding and Don Prues, editors. Writer's Digest Boooks, 1995

Novel and Short Story Writer's Market (Annual), Barbara Kuroff, editor. Writer's Digest Books

Publish Your Own Novel: Get Your Book Into Print and Into the Stores Now!, by Connie Shelton. Columbine Publishing, 1996

The Self-Publishing Manual: How to Write, Print and Sell Your Own Book, 9th Edition, by Dan Poynter. Para Publishing, 1996

Writer's Guide to Book Editors, Publishers and Literary Agents, by Jeff Herman, Jamie Forbes, editor. Prima Publishing, 1996

INDEX

Look for Jean Hager's mystery novels
in your favorite bookstore.

Order Form

Order additional copies of *How to Write & Market Your Mystery Novel* for friends or for classroom use.

Call 1-800-550-7741 to order by credit card

Or copy and mail this form to: Southmont Publishing, P. O. Box 33024, Tulsa, OK 74153-1024

Name_____

Company_____

Address_____

City, ST, Zip_____

Daytime phone_____

_____copies of *How to Write & Market Your Mystery Novel* at $11.95 each   _____
Shipping $3.00 for first book, 50¢
    each additional book   _____
OK residents add 95¢ tax per book   _____
                    Total   _____

Payment:___Check ____Mastercard or Visa (circle one)

Card #_____

Exp.Date_____Signature_____

Or **call 1-800-550-7741** to order now by credit card.
Ask about our quantity discounts on orders of 5 copies or more.